Japanese
and U.S.
Inflation

Japanese and U.S. Inflation

A Comparative Analysis

Ching-yuan Lin
International Monetary Fund

LexingtonBooks
D.C. Heath and Company
Lexington, Massachusetts
Toronto

Library of Congress Cataloging in Publication Data

Lin, Ching-yuan, 1932–
    Japanese and U.S. inflation.

    Includes index.
    1. Inflation (Finance)—United States. 2. Inflation (Finance)—Japan.
3. United States—Economic conditions—1945-   . 4. Japan-Economic
conditions—1945-   . I. Title.
HG540.L55   1984   332.4'1'0952   83–48723
ISBN 0-669-07399-7

Published simultaneously in Canada

Printed in the United States of America

International Standard Book Number: 0-669-07399-7

Library of Congress Catalog Card Number: 83-48723

When the water of Ch'ang Lan is clear,
I can wash the ties of my hat;
When the water of Ch'ang Lan is muddy,
I can (still) wash my feet.

—Folk song quoted in the *Book of Mencius* (386–312, B.C.)

Contents

Contents

Figures

Tables

Acknowledgments

This study was done while I was on one year's sabbatical leave from the International Monetary Fund (IMF). It was prepared mainly at Yale University where I was a Visiting Fellow in the Economic Department and Economic Growth Center during the 1981–1982 academic year.

I thank the IMF Research Department, which allowed me the leave to concentrate on this project, and Yale University, which kindly provided me with the necessary facilities. I am grateful particularly to John Fei, Hugh Patrick, Gustav Ranis, and T.N. Srinivasan for making my association with the Economic Growth Center pleasant and fruitful; to Charles Lindblom and Richard Nelson for allowing me to participate in many seminars held at the Institute of Social and Policy Studies; to James Tobin and William Nordhous for allowing me to audit their classes; and to Albert Fishlow and Colin Bradford for inviting me to the many activities of the Councillium for International Affairs.

In preparing this book, I am indebted to many people, including: Kazuo Sato, New York State University at Buffalo and Columbia University, and Eleanor M. Hadley, George Washington University, for reading and commenting on earlier drafts of all chapters; Hugh Patrick, Yale University, for allowing me to present chapter 4 to the Yale Trade and Development Workshop and to an intercollegiate Japan Economic Seminar held at George Washington University; and Masaru Yoshitomi of Japan's Economic Planning Agency for making my periodic visits to Tokyo fruitful and for exchanging views on the Japanese and the world economy over the years.

I am also grateful for comments I received from the following: George von Furstenburg, International Monetary Fund; Edward Lincoln, U.S.-Japan Trade Council; James Nakamura, Columbia University; Hiroshi Niida, Yokohama National University; Louka T. Katseli Papaefstratiou and T.N. Srinivasan, Yale University; Makoto Sakurai, Japan's Export-Import Bank; Shintaro Takagi, Japan's Seikei University; and several others who attended my seminars. I have also benefited from conversations with Kazushi Ohkawa, formerly of Hitotsubashi University and currently of the International Development Center of Japan; Yoshio Suzuki, Bank of Japan; Hideyoshi Ishiyama, Japan's Ministry of Finance; and Yusuke Onitsuka, Yokohama National University. I thank Wm. C. Hood of the IMF for his kind words and for approving outside publication of this study. Finally, I thank my son Ben for his help in editing an earlier version of various chapters.

Neither the persons mentioned nor the IMF are responsible for the opinions expresed in this book.

1 Introduction

Since the first steep oil price rise in 1973–1974, the world economy has been gripped by the dual problems of persistent inflation and sluggish economic growth. Of the many oil importing countries, only a few have restored the pattern of relatively stable domestic prices and satisfactory economic growth that existed before 1973. Some of them, notably Japan, have restored price stability without regaining a satisfactory rate of economic growth. The great majority, however, have so far failed to restore price stability, with varying performances on real output. Until very recently, the United States belonged to this latter group. (See table 1-1.) Why did inflation subside much earlier in countries like Japan but not in the United States and many others? A focus on Japan and the United States is warranted for a number of reasons.

The United States and Japan are, respectively, the largest and the second largest market economies in the world. Their success or failure in resolving the problem of stagflation eventually has important ramifications for the rest of the world. If the United States cannot restore enduring price stability and continues to pursue stringent monetary policy, the prospect of the world economy's attaining a satisfactory rate of economic growth is not bright. On the other hand, considering the importance of the United States and Japan as markets for world exports, the way by which price stability is restored is also important. The rest of the world—in particular, the developing countries—does not wish to see the United States and Japan restore price stability by means of severely deflating their economies and consequently depressing their import demand for a prolonged period of time.

The United States and Japan are each other's principal overseas trading partner.[1] If economic conditions between the two countries diverge widely, disequilibrium in their bilateral trade balance becomes severe, causing wide exchange rate fluctuations and intensified protectionist sentiments, the latter particuarly on the part of the United States. The resulting impact affects not only the two major protagonists but also many other smaller countries trading with them. This has happened twice: in the late 1960s in the aftermath of the Vietnam war and again in the late 1970s after the 1973–1974 oil shock. In fact, one may even speculate that the Bretton Woods system of fixed exchange rates might have lasted longer (this does not mean that it should have) had the disequilibrium in the trade balance between the United States and Japan in the late 1960s not been as severe as it was.

1

Table 1-1
Deviations of the Rate of Growth of Real Output and of the Rate of Inflation after 1974 Compared to Pre-1974 Periods, Oil Importing Countries
(annual percentage changes)

	Growth of Real Output				Rate of Inflation[a]			
	1963–1973	1973–1980	1978–1980	Ratio of 1973–1980 Rate over 1963–1973	1967–1972	1974	1978–1980	Ratio of 1978–1980 Rate over 1967–1972
Industrial Countries[b]	4.9	2.5	2.5	0.51	4.1	11.6	8.4	2.0
United States	4.0	2.3	1.5	0.58	3.6	8.7	8.8	2.4
Japan	10.4	4.3	4.9	0.41	5.0	20.0	2.8	0.6
Germany, Federal Republic of	4.5	2.4	3.2	0.53	4.0	6.8	4.5	1.1
France	5.5	2.8	2.4	0.51	4.8	11.1	10.9	2.3
Italy	4.7	2.8	4.5	0.60	5.1	18.3	18.1	3.6
United Kingdom	3.2	0.8	—	0.25	5.2	15.0	16.8	3.2
Nonoil developing countries[c]	5.9[d]	5.0	4.7	0.85	9.1	28.7	33.3	3.7
Net oil exporters[e]	6.3[d]	5.6	6.9	0.89	4.1	20.6	21.2	5.2
Net oil importers	5.8[d]	4.8	4.3	0.83	10.0	30.2	35.7	3.6

Sources: International Monetary Fund, *World Economic Outlook* (June 1981) and *International Financial Statistics* (various issues).

[a] GNP deflator for industrial countries and consumer prices for nonoil developing countries. The latter is based on geometric average weighted by GDP. Shown as the compound rate of changes between the beginning and the last year.

[b] Includes, in addition to countries listed, the following: Australia, Austria, Belgium, Canada, Denmark, Finland, Iceland, Ireland, Luxembourg, Netherlands, New Zealand, Norway, Spain, Sweden, and Switzerland.

[c] Excluding People's Republic of China. Includes all members of the IMF except the industrial countries.

[d] For 1967–1973.

[e] Includes Bahrain, Bolivia, the People's Republic of the Congo, Ecuador, Egypt, Gabon, Malaysia, Mexico, Peru, Syria, Trinidad and Tobago, and Tunisia.

During the worldwide acceleration of inflation in 1973–1974, Japan experienced a much sharper upsurge in prices than did the United States. From 4 to 6 percent rates of increase in the preceding two years, the rise in Japanese consumer prices speeded up to 11.8 percent in 1973 and 24.3 percent in 1974. In comparison, the U.S. consumer price index increased only 6.3 percent in 1973 and 10.9 percent in 1974, following a rate of 3 to 4 percent in the preceding two years. Yet in the ensuing years, the Japanese inflation rate has gradually declined despite the second oil shock of 1979–1980 while U.S. inflation, following a spell of improvement in 1975–1976, subsequently worsened. In terms of a composite deflator for gross national product (GNP), Japanese factor prices increased by only 2.8 percent per year in 1979–1980 compared to a peak rate of 20 percent in 1974 and an average of 5 percent per year in the five years ended in 1972. By contrast, the U.S. GNP deflator rose by 8.8 percent per annum in 1979–1980, about the same rate as in 1974 and nearly two and a half times the average annual rate between 1967 and 1972. (See table 1–1 and figure 1–1).

What has caused this divergence in economic experience? Why did inflation subside in Japan in the aftermath of the first oil shock and subsequent recession, while the inflation rate turned up again in the United States following an initial decline? Was Japanese price stability attributable mainly to its protracted recession, while resurgence in U.S. inflation was a consequence of its much faster recovery from the 1974–1975 recession? And, if so, was the Japanese price stabilization attained at the cost of great losses in output and income (compared to Japan's potential growth rate) and, hence, is not worthy of emulation, or is some part of the Japanese experience relevant to the U.S. situation?

In order to answer these questions, we must examine the evolution of the two economies both before and after 1974 and their respective government's policy responses to the repeated price shocks. This may enable us to see whether government actions exacerbated the situation or ameliorated it. The following questions need to be answered: what are the effects of external price shocks, and what government policy responses are appropriate? Should these responses differ from the case where the acceleration in inflation originates from an excess demand condition in the domestic economy?

If the acceleration in inflation originates from an excess demand condition in the domestic economy, such as at the peak of a business cycle, there is no doubt that the appropriate government policy response should be a tightening of both fiscal and monetary policies, even though there are controversies with regard to their effectiveness as a countercyclical policy tool. Such controversies are concerned mostly with the difficulty of timing the implementation of the required policy actions as well as the long-run offset to the effects of these polices. There is little question that if the timing is right, a restrictive monetary and fiscal policy would help in restoring both

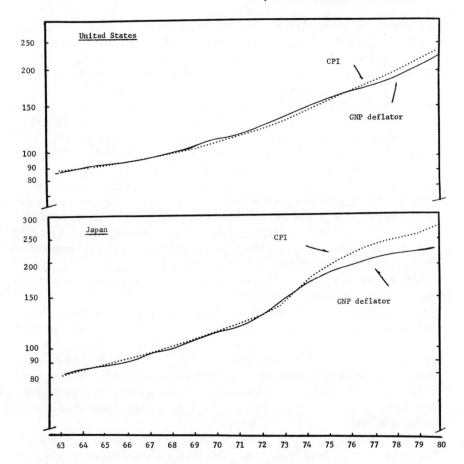

Figure 1-1. Indexes of Consumer Prices and GNP Deflator, 1963–1980
        (1967 = 100)

internal and exernal balance to an over-active economy. This is not
necessarily true, however, if the acceleration in price inflation is caused by a
quantum jump in import prices. Under such a situation, a tightening of
monetary policy exacerbates the delationary impact of the rise in import
prices and that of the worsened external balance. This leads to undue losses
in output, income, and employment, without a direct impact on the cost-
push effect of increased import costs. This is illustrated in figure 1-2.

    Suppose that the supply curve for real gross domestic product (GDP) is
upward sloping and the agregate demand curve is downward sloping in a
coordinate where the abscissa indicates real output and the ordinate price
level.[2] Assume further that a quantum jump in import prices shifts both the

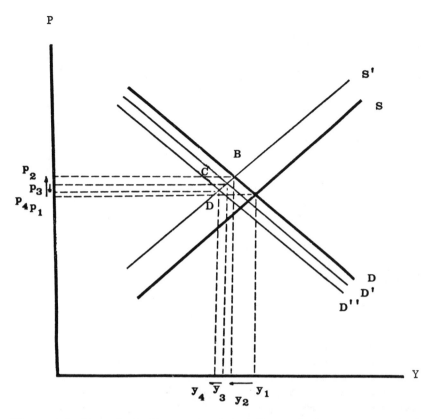

Figure 1-2. Hypothetical Example of the Effects of a Large Increase in Oil Import Price on the Supply and Demand of Gross Domestic Product and the Effects of a Tightening in Monetary Policy in Response to Externally Originated Inflation

supply and the demand curves. The supply curve shifts because of a rise in the costs of materials, fuels, and wages. The demand curve shifts because of losses in purchasing power caused by the higher cost of living, a rise in interest rates caused by the increased demand for money in nominal terms but reduced supply of it in real terms, and weakened inventory demand associated with reduced final demand and increased financial cost. To some extent, the inward shift in the demand curve is offset by the automatic stabilizing effect of reduced payments for income taxes (although this part of the effect may be weakened by an increase in the tax base caused by the inflation) and increased income transfers under the social security system. The inward shift of the supply curve raises supply cost for a given level of real output, while the inward shift of the demand curve reduces the amount of real output demanded at a given price level. The new equilibrium, say, at point C, may have a smaller output (Y_3) with a higher price level (P_3). If the authorities tighten the monetary policy, output may fall further to point Y_4, although the price level may go lower.

To avoid falling into this pit of stagflation, the authorities may take a series of policies and measures whose combined effects are to shift the supply curve backward to the right. Such a shift can take place with the aid of the following: a moderation in wage demands, which will increase in response to the rise in cost of living caused by the higher import costs; a substitution away from imported fuels or other materials whose costs have risen; and an improved productivity performance over time. Moderation of wage demands, tantamount to a cutback in real wages, can take place only if it is in exchange for the maintenance of employment, which otherwise will decline. To this effect, the government can promote labor-management cooperation by means of direct intervention in the wage negotiation process or through granting tax incentives (such as a temporary cutback in payroll taxes) to the businesses that would otherwise lay off workers. Substitution of imported fuels or materials can be promoted through the use of tax incentives, but this may contribute less toward productivity improvements than toward restoring the external balance. Improving productivity under external price shocks is not an easy task, but the governemt can aid this by using tax incentives in maintaining investment demand and capacity utilization. In the short run the pursuit of restrictive monetary policy in response to an external price shock works against the maintenance of capacity utilization and productivity growth because of its depressive effect on the growth of domestic demand.

In the light of these arguments, we can examine in detail the causes of divergence in price stabilization in the United States and Japan, focusing on the interaction between government policy and the evolution of the economy. The questions to be answered are grouped in the following manner.

1. What was the reaction of each respective government to the first oil shock in terms of fiscal and monetary policies? Was the protracted recession in Japan attributable largely to the fact that monetary policy was held tight much longer in Japan than in the United States, or was there a basic worsening in Japanese economic conditions that was not as evident for U.S. businesses? How did economic conditions evolve in the United States and Japan between the first and the second oil shock? What was the response of the authorities in the two countries to the second oil shock? Was there any significant change in the respective government's policy responses to external price shocks between the first and the second oil shock? Why, after the second oil shock, did inflation stabilize quickly in Japan and accelerate in the United States? Was the divergence in price stabilization attributable to

differences in macroecomomic policy or to differences in underlying economic conditions?

2. How did wages, labor productivity, and unit labor costs behave in the two countries before and after the 1974–1975 disturbances? Was the success of price stabilization in Japan accompanied by a marked slowdown in the rise of unit labor costs? Was there a marked slowdown of wage demands in Japan in the aftermath of the 1974–1975 recession but not in the United States? What causes the divergence in wage behavior in the two countries: differences in underlying economic conditions or other factors, such as differences in the employment system and unionism? Why was the growth of labor productivity much faster in Japan than in the United States both before and after the 1974–1975 disturbances? Was it due to a rapid growth of capital stock per worker in Japan? If so, how was Japanese productivity performance maintained in the wake of investment slowdown after 1974–1975?

3. How was Japan able to maintain a high rate of household saving both before and after 1974–1975? Why did Japanese personal saving remain at a high level despite a marked slowdown in the growth of disposal income, while U.S. personal saving declined in the more recent years? What was the role of the Japanese government in the financial intermediation of the saving and investment process? How did sectoral saving-investment balances change in the aftermath of the 1974–1975 disturbances? Was there a major difference in the financing of fiscal deficit in the two countries? Why was the smaller fiscal deficit (in relation to the size of the economy) perennially preceived as a threat to American financial stability, while the growing and larger Japanese fiscal deficit has not caused great financial difficulties?

These are the questions this book seeks to answer. Chapter 2 provides an overview of inflation and the process of price stabilization in the two countries in the past decade. Five subperiods are outlined: (1) the late 1960s when productivity and price trends in the two countries started to deviate; (2) 1971–1973 when worsening U.S. economic performance was temporarily halted by wage-price controls and the termination of the Bretton Woods system of adjustable pegs while investment climate in Japan deteriorated because of sharp currency appreciation and increasingly tight labor supply; (3) 1974–1975 when both countries suffered severe terms of trade losses from the quantum jumps in oil prices; (4) 1976–1978 when price trends in the two countries deviated again because of differences in the tempo of economic recovery and divergent wage and productivity behavior; and (5) 1979–1980 when the impacts of the second oil shock on the two economies turned out differently because of underlying differences in economic conditions.

Chapter 3 examines the management of monetary and fiscal policy in response to the two oil shocks. It focuses on causes of the protracted recession in Japan in the aftermath of the first oil shock and the role of monetary restraints; the evolution of fiscal receipts and expenditures in the two countries; external impacts of Japan's protracted recession, especially on its trade balance with the United States; and macropolicy responses to the second oil shock in the light of the experience from the first oil shock. On the last item, special attention is paid to impacts of the changed monetary rule in the United States since 1979.

Chapter 4 examines the movements of wage rate, unit labor costs, and finished goods prices in manufacturing both before and after the oil shock and discusses the factors underlying divergent wage behavior in the two countries. Attention is paid especially to differences in their employment systems and unionism, which made Japanese employment less responsive to, and their wage rates more responsive to, cyclical changes in economic activity than did U.S. counterparts. Also considered is the variation in wage and price behavior between large corporations and the small business sector in Japan. Finally, the merits and demerits of the employment system in the two countries are assessed with respect to their contribution to macroeconomic performance.

Chapter 5 examines the major factors underlying the contrasting productivity trends in the two countries both before and after the oil shock. Attention is paid to differences in the growth of capital stock per employee and the evolution of capital-output ratio. The divergence in investment and productivity behavior is explained with reference to differences in economic conditions in the two countries both before and after the oil shock. Also emphasized are the Japanese knack for improvements over imported technologies and the high motivations of Japanese workers in comparison with their American counterparts.

Chapter 6 examines changes in saving-investment balance between the three major sectors, households, corporate businesses, and the government, and attempts to explain the extremely high saving propensity of Japanese households relative to that of their U.S. counterparts, the role of the Japanese government in the financial intermediation of saving and investment, and the reasons that the smaller U.S. fiscal deficit (in relation to GNP) is perennially perceived as a threat to financial stability while the larger Japanese deficit did not aggravate inflation. The last chapter summarizes the major findings of this study.

Notes

1. The United States is Japan's largest trading partner, whereas Japan is the United States's second largest trading partner, next only to the neighboring Canada.

2. The aggregate supply curve is upward sloping because wages and prices are assumed to be neither perfectly flexible nor completely inflexible. The aggregate demand curve is downward sloping because a given quantity of money supply can support a higher level of aggregate demand for labor when prices are lower and the real money stock is greater. For these assumptions and analyses on alternative policy responses to external price shocks, see Robert J. Gordon, "Alternative Responses of Policy to External Supply Shocks," *Brookings Papers on Economic Activity* (1:1975); Edmund S. Phelps, "Commodity Supply Shock and Full Employment Monetary Policy," *Journal of Money, Credit and Banking* 10 (May 1978); Edward M. Gramlich, "Macro Policy Responses to Price Shocks," *Brookings Papers on Economic Activity* (1:1979). For alternative assumptions or views, see Robert H. Rasche and John A. Tatom, "The Price Shocks, Aggregate Supply and Monetary Policy: The Theory and International Evidence," in Karl Brunner and Alan H. Meltzer, eds., *Supply Shocks, Incentives, and National Wealth*, Carnegie Rochester Conference Series on Public Policy, 14 (Amsterdam: North Holland, 1981), and Knut Anton Mork and Robert E. Hall, "Energy Prices, Inflation, and Recession, 1974–75," MIT Working Paper No. MITEL 79 028WP (Cambridge: MIT, August 1979). For the distinction between the effect of a rise in the import price of intermediate goods and that of final goods, as well as between that of imports complementary to domestic goods versus those that are gross substitutes, see Louka T. Katseli Papaefstratiou, "Transmission of External Price Disturbances and the Composition of Trade," *Journal of International Economics* 10 (1980):357–375.

2 An Overview of Inflation and the Process of Stabilization, 1965–1980

In retrospect, one can see that what happened after 1974 in terms of both government policy response and business behavior was very much predicated on economic experiences before the oil shock. Therefore, in order to understand and to compare the pattern of economic development and inflation between the United States and Japan, we need to examine the events and developments leading to the 1973–1974 disturbances. An appropriate starting point is the second half of the 1960s, the period when major economic trends in the two countries (particularly with respect to productivity growth) began to deviate substantially. The second subperiod is the early 1970s when one of the major constraints on balance-of-payments adjustment between the two countries, the Bretton Woods system of fixed exchange rates, was finally removed and when both the United States and many of its major trading partners attempted to inflate their domestic economies in the aftermath of the 1970–1971 recession.

The years after the first oil shock can also be subdivided into distinct periods because of various developments. The first subperiod is 1974–1975 when both countries suffered severe terms of trade losses and when their governments implemented similar demand management policies. Another subperiod encompasses the years from 1976 to 1978 when developments in both countries began to deviate again. The last subperiod is 1979–1980 when the second oil shock struck, and its impact, as distinct from the situation in 1974–1975, differed widely between the two countries as a consequence of cumulative differences in economic developments and private and public economic behavior since 1974.

Divergence of Productivity and Price Trends, Late 1960s

Divergence in price and output performance between the United States and Japan can be traced to economic events in the late 1960s. For the United States, the growth of inflationary forces already was evident from the mid-1960s in conjunction with the excess demand conditions caused by the Vietnam war and a sharp slowdown in productivity growth. In contrast,

11

Japan was experiencing a sharp acceleration in productivity growth and output during the same period. Although real wages increased much faster in Japan than in the United States, this was offset by the rapid productivity growth. The acceleration of inflation did not become evident in Japan until 1973 (figures 2-1 and 2-2).[1]

This divergence in productivity and price trends, in conjunction with the excess demand condition then existing in the United States, caused the bilateral trade balance between the two countries to move strongly in Japan's favor. This in turn caused severe strains on the dollar-yen parity, which was fixed under the Bretton Woods system.

Until the mid-1960s, growth of labor productivity was actually very satisfactory in the United States. Unit labor costs were relatively stable. During the first half of the decade, output per man-hour in the private business sector increased 3.8 percent per year, while unit labor costs rose only 0.4 percent per year.[2] However, during the next five years, the rise in output per man-hour decelerated to a mere 1.9 percent per year, while the rise in unit labor costs accelerated to as much as 4.8 percent per year.

What caused the sudden decline in productivity growth and a concomitant rise in unit labor costs in the United States? As distinct from the situation in the 1970s, there was neither a deterioration in the terms of trade nor a severe underutilization of productive capacities. On the contrary, the terms of trade were favorable, and wholesale prices of crude materials, including crude oil, remained largely stable except for a brief flare-up in 1965-1966. Rather the evidence points to the strong demand pressures caused by the expansion of defense expenditures in the midst of an already rapidly growing economy. In fact, from 1961 to 1967, private domestic demand increased by 4.9 percent per year in real terms, compared to 2.7 percent per year in the preceding decade. Gross domestic investment increased by 6.4 percent per year compared to the earlier growth rate of a mere 1.2 percent per year. In addition, government purchases of goods and services were expanding at an annual rate of nearly 9 percent per year in real terms from 1965 to 1967, a consequence of the escalation of war efforts in Vietnam.

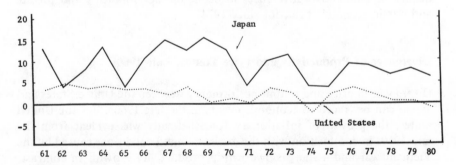

Figure 2-1. Changes in Real Output per Man-Hour in Manufacturing, 1961-1980 (annual percentage changes)

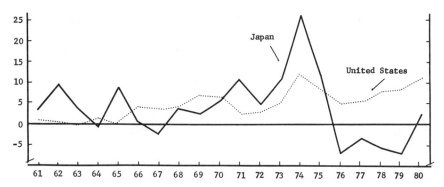

Figure 2-2. Changes in Unit Labor Costs in Manufacturing, 1961–1980 (annual percentage changes in national currency units)

The results were a tightened labor market situation and the generation of cost-push pressures despite an accelerated growth of productive capacities and employment. From 1960 to 1969, total civilian employment increased by 2.1 percent per year compared to a mere 0.9 percent per year in the preceding decade. The unemployment rate of the civilian labor force had declined from 6.7 percent in 1961 to 3.5 percent in 1969, and the rate of capacity utilization in the manufacturing sector, based on the Federal Reserve series, exceeded the critical 90 percentile in 1966 before declining somewhat in the next few years. In consequence, the increases in compensation per hour for the private business sector[3] accelerated, from 4.2 percent per year in the first half of the 1960s to 6.8 percent per year in the second half.

Although the acceleration in wage increases can be explained by a much tightened labor market situation, the causes of the productivity slowdown are less apparent. Part of this decline may be explained by the end-of-expansion phenomenon of 1969, when businesses increased hiring not knowing that demand would soon peak.[4] The expansion of defense spending may have distorted the composition of incremental productive capacities, which then became excessive when the war efforts wound down. Output growth for certain industries may have been unfavorably affected by intense foreign competition under the fixed exchange rate. Because of the tendency for wage adjustments in the declining industries to catch up with the growing industries under collective bargaining, the competitive position of the declining industries may have further declined, thereby entering a vicious circle.

In addition, the second half of the 1960s also witnessed an acceleration in the growth of female participation in the labor force. Contrary to the trend of the male participation rate, which continued to decline (from 86.4 percent in 1950 to 83.3 percent in 1960 and 79.7 percent in 1970), the female participation rate increased by 9.4 percentage points in twenty years (from less than 34 percent to over 43 percent in 1970), with a gain of 4 percentage points in the second half of the 1970s (figure 2-3). For men, the biggest drop in participation rate occurred among those aged fifty-five and over, attributable primarily to improved pension benefits for early retirement. For women whose participation rate increased for the child-bearing age groups from age twenty to age forty (table 2-1), the causes were many and complex, including such factors as the changed social attitude toward working women, reduced family size, increased years of education, and increased job opportunities.[5] The expansion of the Vietnam war in 1966-1967 during which 4 million men were enlisted and the rapid expansion of the service sectors created increased job opportunities for women.[6]

In sharp contrast with the worsened cost-price relationship in the United States, the rise in unit labor costs slowed down markedly in Japan in the second half of the 1960s because a sharper acceleration in productivity growth was offset only partially by a much smaller acceleration in the rate of increase of wage costs. Thus, during the second half of the 1960s, real output per man-hour in Japan's manufacturing sector increased by more than 13 percent per year against 8.5 percent per year in the first half. During the corresponding five-year periods, the annual rate of increase of employee compensation accelerated only from 13.4 percent to 15.0 percent, resulting in a decline in the annual rate of increase of unit labor costs from 4.5 percent to 1.7 percent.

Why was Japan able to sustain such a high rate of productivity growth? A source-of-growth analysis by factor inputs indicated marked increases in capital stock per unit of labor and in the residual factors (which were attrib-

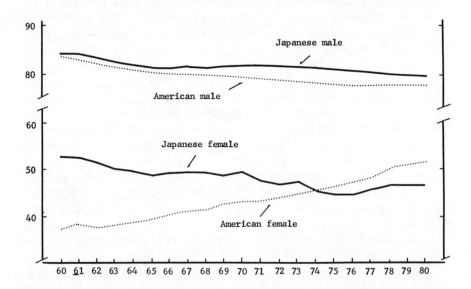

Figure 2-3. Male and Female Labor Force Participation Rate, 1960-1980
(percentages)

Table 2-1
Female Labor Force Participation Rate by Age Groups, 1960–1980
(percentages)

	Total, 15 or 16 years Old or Over[a]	16-17	17-19 (15-19)[b]	20-24	25-29	30-34	35-39 (35-44)[c]	40-54 (45-54)[c]	55-59 (55-64)[c]	60-64	65 and Over
United States											
1955	35.7	28.9	51.0	46.0	34.9		41.6	43.8	32.5		10.8
1960	37.8	29.1	51.1	46.2	36.0		43.5	49.8	37.2		10.8
1965	39.3	27.7	49.4	50.0	38.6		46.1	50.9	41.1		10.0
1970	43.4	34.9	53.7	57.8	45.0		51.1	54.4	43.0		9.7
1975	46.4	40.2	58.3	64.3	54.6		55.8	54.6	41.0		8.3
1979	51.1	45.8	63.1	69.3	63.9		63.8	58.4	41.9		8.3
Changes											
1955-1979	15.4	16.9	12.1	23.3	29.0		22.2	14.6	9.4		-2.5
1965-1970	4.1	7.2	4.3	7.8	6.4		5.0	3.5	1.9		-0.3
1970-1979	7.7	10.9	9.4	11.5	18.9		12.7	4.0	-1.1		-1.4
Japan											
1960	54.5		49.0	70.8	54.5	56.5	59.0	59.0	49.7	43.0	25.6
1965	50.6		35.8	70.2	49.0	51.1	59.6	60.2	49.8	39.8	21.6
1970	49.9		33.6	70.6	45.5	48.2	57.5	61.8	44.3		17.9
1975	45.7		21.7	66.2	42.6	43.9	54.0	59.9	48.8	38.0	15.3
1980	47.6		18.5	70.0	49.2	48.2	58.0	62.8	50.5	38.0	15.5
Changes											
1960-1970	-4.6		-15.4	-0.2	-9.0	-8.3	-1.5	2.2			-8.3
1970-1975	-4.2		-11.9	-4.4	-2.9	-4.3	-3.5	-1.9			-2.6
1975-1980	1.9		-3.2	3.8	6.6	4.3	4.0	2.9	1.7		0.2

Sources: United States: Department of Labor, *Handbook of Labor Statistics* (December 1980); Japan: Prime Minister's Office, *Japan Statistical Yearbook* (various issues).

[a]15 years old and over for Japan; 16 years old and over for the United States.

[b]For Japan.

[c]For the United States.

utable primarily to technical progress) throughout the 1960s, while the growth of employment and the shift of capital and labor from the low-productivity sectors to high-productivity sectors made positive but diminishing contributions to the growth of real output.[7] A sustained high rate of investment in Japan was made possible by a number of factors, including favorable government policies and institutional arrangements, the abundance of investment opportunities for catching up with the United States in advanced technology and consumption patterns, and the rapid growth of export demand in a favorable world economic environment. During the 1960s Japan's export volume increased by around 17 percent per year while real domestic demand increased by less than 11 percent per year. Thus, in real terms, there was a continuing increase in the share of exports of goods and services in GNP despite a fluctuating, largely unchanged export share in current prices (table 2–2).

The contribution of export expansion to Japan's economic growth was also manifest in a continued large trade surplus in the second half of the 1960s. By removing the balance-of-payments constraint on sustained expansion of domestic demand, the latter facilitated trend acceleration of Japan's economic growth rate.[8] The structural change in Japan's balance of payments was the cumulative result of continuing improvements in Japanese industry's competitive position in the world markets, but it was expedited also by a worsening in the relative cost position of U.S. industry. As the accelerated increase in U.S. industry's unit labor costs occurred at a

Table 2–2
Growth of Japanese Real GNP and Export Volume and Exports of Goods and Services, and Trade Balance in Relation to GNP, 1952–1980
(percentage changes)

| | Growth of | | | Share of GNP[a] | |
	Real GNP (1)	Export Volume (2)	Ratio (2)/(1) (3)	Exports of Goods and Services (4)	Trade Balance (5)
1952–1960	7.0	17.0	2.4	11.7	0.1
1960–1970	11.1	17.2	1.5	10.5	0.2
1970–1980	5.1	9.6	1.9	13.0	0.5
1960–1965	10.0	19.5	1.9	10.1	−0.6
1965–1970	12.2	15.0	1.2	10.8	0.9
1970–1973	8.2	10.5	1.3	11.4	1.2
1973–1975	0.4	9.3	23.3	14.1	−0.5
1975–1978	5.9	7.0	1.2	13.4	1.3
1978–1980	4.9	7.5	1.5	14.0	−0.9

Source: International Monetary Fund, *International Financial Statistics* (various issues).
[a]Not including the beginning years shown in the stub.

time when there was a marked slowdown in the increase of unit labor costs in Japan, the relative cost position between the industries in the two countries changed drastically in favor of Japanese industry during the second half of the 1960s. From 1965 to 1970, U.S. industry's unit labor costs rose over 12 percent more than their Japanese counterparts.

This change in relative cost position could have been offset by movements in the exchange rate; however, because of the difficulty for the key currency to devalue under the Bretton Woods system and the reluctance of the Japanese authorities to revalue the yen, Japanese exports to the United States expanded at a rate faster than the growth of its total exports while Japan's imports from the United States increased at a rate slower than the growth of its total imports. This resulted in a sharp improvement of Japan's trade balance with the United States, which has become a constant feature of the two countries' trade relations (table 2-3).

1971-1973 Currency Realignments and U.S. Wage-Price Controls

The impasse was broken only after huge outflows of U.S. dollars prompted President Nixon to terminate the U.S. dollar's gold convertibility on August 15, 1971, while also imposing a 10 percent import surcharge and a temporary freeze on wages, prices, and rents. Until their removal on April 30, 1974, the wage and price controls underwent four phases with shifting restrictiveness and achieving limited success in reducing inflation in 1972-1973. According to simulations performed by a Data Resources model, without controls, both the U.S. GNP deflator and consumer price index would have been 1.3 percent higher by the fourth quarter of 1973 and the wholesale price would have been 3.4 percent higher.[9]

In addition to the restraint on wage increases, U.S. industries were also helped by an effective devaluation of the U.S. dollar of nearly 15 percent between 1970 and 1973.[10] As a result, the U.S. relative cost position improved, and, spurred by expanding demand both at home and abroad, the declining trend of labor productivity was reversed temporarily. (See figures 2-1 and 2-2 and table 4-1.) However, during both 1972 and 1973 the prices of agricultural products rose rapidly as a result of a combination of poor harvests, diminished stocks, and increased world demand. The prices of other primary products, stimulated by worldwide speculative demand, also rose in sympathy, albeit at varying rates. Within two years the U.S. wholesale price index for crude materials had risen 51 percent, while the food subindex of the consumer price index rose over 19 percent (figure 2-4).[11]

Meanwhile, Japan's reluctance to revalue its currency (and its eagerness to stimulate the domestic economy) contributed to a sharp expansion of the

Table 2-3
Trade Balances with Selected Trading Partners, 1966–1980
(billions of U.S. dollars, for annual averages)

	Japan						United States			
	Trade with						Trade with			
					Nonoil LDCS[a]					
	Total Trade	United States	Other Industrial Countries	Major Oil Exporters	In Asia	Other Areas	Total Trade	Japan	Major Oil Exporters	Other Countries
1966–1970	0.1	0.4					1.1	−0.9		
1971–1973	2.7	2.0	1.0	−3.2	2.5	0.2	−5.2	−3.4	−0.4	−1.2
1974–1975	−4.3	−0.1	1.5	−13.3	3.3	1.8	−6.9	−2.7	−8.6	4.4
1976–1978	10.2	7.4	5.7	−13.6	5.7	2.7	−30.1	−10.1	−19.2	−1.4
1979–1980	−9.2	6.7	1.8	−31.9	5.9	3.6	−34.7	−11.4	−33.4	10.1

Sources: International Monetary Fund, *International Financial Statistics* and *Direction of Trade* (various issues).

Note: Exports are valued f.o.b. and imports c.i.f.

[a]LDCs = less developed countries.

Percent

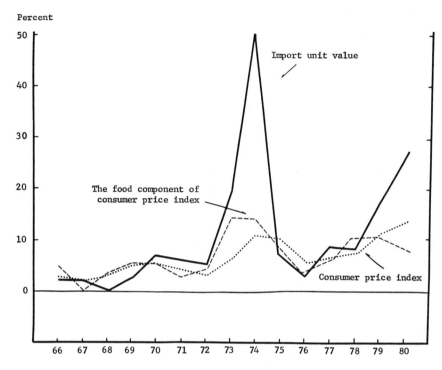

Figure 2-4. Annual Changes in U.S. Consumer Price Index and Subindex for Its Food Component, and Import Unit Value, 1966-1980

money supply during 1971–1972 through the monetary authorities' acquisitions of foreign assets. Such acquisitions amounted to 49 percent in 1971 and 12.5 percent in 1972, of the preceding year's stock of base money, while the money supply (M1) expanded by around 30 percent and 25 percent, respectively. This compares with an average monetary growth rate of 18 percent in the preceding decade (figure 2–5). The sharp expansion of liquidity fueled speculative purchases of commodities, land, and miscellaneous collectibles in 1973–1974 when the Japanese public was gripped by fears of potential commodity shortages and strong price expectations under the condition of worldwide economic booms.

Well before that, however, Japanese industry's relative cost position showed evidence of deterioration because of the combination of a slowdown in productivity growth, a stepped-up increase in employee compensation, and a sizable revaluation of the yen. In the three years from 1970 to 1973, output per man-hour in the manufacturing sector increased 8.5 percent per year compared to more than 13 percent per year in the preceding five years, and compensation per man-hour increased by nearly 18 percent

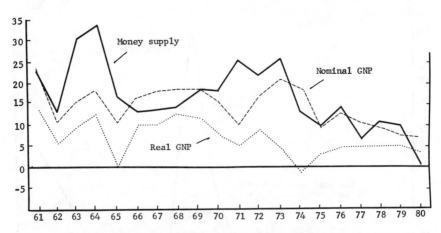

Figure 2-5. Japan's Growth of Money Supply (M1) and Nominal and Real GNP, 1960–1980 (annual percentage changes)

per year compared to 15 percent per year in the corresponding periods. As a result, the unit labor costs increased by 8.7 percent per year compared to only 2.7 percent per year in the preceding five years. Meanwhile the yen appreciated by 32 percent against the U.S. dollar and by nearly 23 percent in effective rate. In terms of U.S. dollars, Japanese unit labor costs rose by as much as 70 percent from 1970 to 1973 against an increase of only 5.8 percent for the U.S. counterpart.

The stepped-up increase in employee compensation, which occurred despite the productivity slowdown, resulted from a progressive tightening of labor markets over more than a decade of accelerated economic growth. For the decade ending in 1973, the Japanese labor force grew by only 1.3 percent per year (compared to 2.0 percent per year in the United States), partly because of a steady decline in the labor force participation rate. Contrary to trends in the United States, the female participation rate had continued to decline during the postwar decades, from over 55 percent in the 1950s to about 45 percent in the mid-1970s (figure 2-3 and table 2-1). The decline in the Japanese female participation rate occurred in conjunction with a sharp decline in the labor force engaged in agricultural activity and a steady increase until 1975 in the ratio of women engaged in housekeeping (table 2-4). The former was offset to a large extent by increased employment of female workers in secondary and tertiary activities. The latter was reflected in the continuous decline, until the mid-1970s, in the labor force participation rate of women in the prime child-bearing ages of twenty-five to thirty-four (table 2-1). This contrasted sharply with the situation in the United States where the labor force participation rate of child-bearing age groups increased rapidly from the mid-1960s onward.

Table 2-4
Selected Data on Japanese Female Employment, 1955–1980

	Female Population, 15 Years Old or Over	Female Labor Force	Female Employment						
			Total	Unpaid Family Workers	Self-Employed	Employees	Engaged in Agriculture and Forestry Activity	Totally Unemployed	Mainly Housekeeping
Number (in 10,000)									
1955	3,068	1,740	1,705	965	246	492	823	34	
1960	3,370	1,838	1,812	842	273	695	733	26	1,005
1965	3,758	1,903	1,883	744	265	873	622	21	1,188
1970	4,060	2,024	2,003	619	285	1,096	442	21	1,373
1973	4,239	2,045	2,021	523	309	1,186	345	24	1,493
1975	4,331	1,983	1,953	501	280	1,167	322	34	1,603
1978	4,487	2,125	2,083	512	287	1,280	301	43	1,550
1980	4,591	2,185	2,142	491	293	1,354	272	43	1,560
Composition (percentages)									
1955	100.0	56.9	55.6	31.5	8.0	16.0	26.8	1.1	
1960	100.0	54.5	53.7	25.0	8.1	20.6	21.8	.8	29.8
1965	100.0	50.6	50.1	19.8	7.1	23.2	16.6	.6	31.6
1970	100.0	49.9	49.3	15.2	7.0	27.0	10.9	.5	33.8
1973	100.0	48.2	46.7	12.3	7.3	28.0	8.1	.6	35.2
1975	100.0	45.8	45.1	11.6	6.5	26.9	7.4	.8	37.0
1978	100.0	47.3	46.4	11.4	6.4	28.5	6.7	1.0	34.5
1980	100.0	47.6	46.7	10.7	6.4	29.5	5.9	.9	34.0
Changes									
1955–1973		-8.7	-8.9	-19.2	-.7	12.0	-18.7	-.5	4.4[a]
1973–1975		-2.4	-1.6	-.7	-.8	-1.1	-.7	.2	1.8
1975–1980		1.8	1.6	-.9	-.1	2.6	1.5	.1	-3.0

Source: Japanese Prime Minister's Office, *Japan Statistical Yearbook* (various issues).
[a]Changes in 1973 over 1960.

During this period the unemployment rate in Japan declined from over 2 percent of the labor force in the late 1950s to between 1.1 and 1.3 percent at the beginning of the 1970s. The ratio of job offers to job applications registered in the nation's employment service offices rose from 0.6 to 0.8 in the mid-1960s to 1.1 to 1.4 in the early 1970s, despite a continuous, albeit decelerating transfer of labor from agricultural to nonagricultural sectors.

Impacts of the 1973–1974 Oil Shock and Terms of Trade Loss

Because of Japan's heavy reliance on foreign supplies of fuels and raw materials, the country suffered a much greater loss in terms of trade from the quantum jumps in oil prices than did the United States. The Japanese loss in terms of trade amounted to more than 25 percent in 1974, about 10 percent more than for the United States. Based on the amount of exports in the preceding year, the Japanese loss was equivalent to 2.0 percent of the country's GNP in 1974. For the United States, which is less reliant on foreign trade, the 1974 loss in terms of trade was equivalent to 1.1 percent of GNP (table 2–5). Moreover, the 1974 jump in Japanese import unit values was not only higher than in the United States (70 percent versus 50 percent) in dollar terms but even more so in yen terms (84 percent) because of currency depreciation in the aftermath of the oil shock (figures 2–6 and 2–7).

Table 2–5
Changes in Terms of Trade in Relation to GNP, 1971–1980
(percentages)

	Changes in Terms of Trade		Changes in Terms of Trade in Relation to GNP[a]	
	United States	*Japan*	*United States*	*Japan*
1971	−2.8	2.9	−0.1	0.3
1972	−4.1	4.5	−.2	.4
1973	−2.1	−4.6	−.1	−.3
1974	−15.3	−25.4	−1.1	−2.0
1975	4.6	−5.0	.3	−.6
1976	1.0	−3.9	.1	−.4
1977	4.4	3.1	.3	.3
1978	−.5	16.5		1.4
1979	−.7	−15.2	−.1	−1.5
1980	−13.4	−20.2	−.9	−2.0
1974–1980	−2.8	−7.2	−.2	−.7

Sources: Author's estimate from International Monetary Fund, *International Financial Statistics* (various issues).

[a]Estimated as: (percentage change in terms of trade) × (preceding year's export value) ÷ (GNP) × 100.

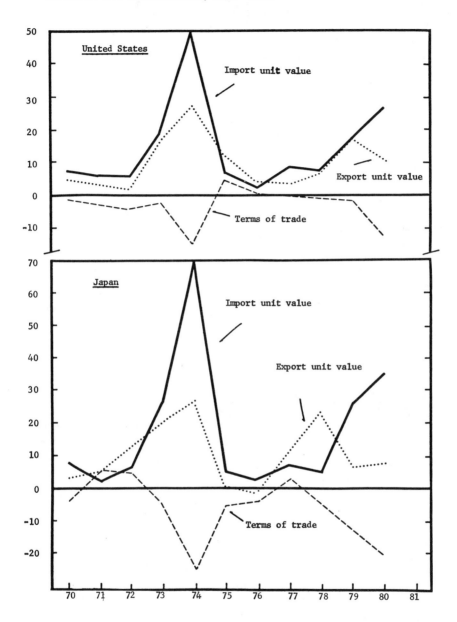

Figure 2-6. Annual Changes in Export Unit Value, Import Unit Value, and Terms of Trade, 1970–1980 (percentages, in terms of U.S. dollars)

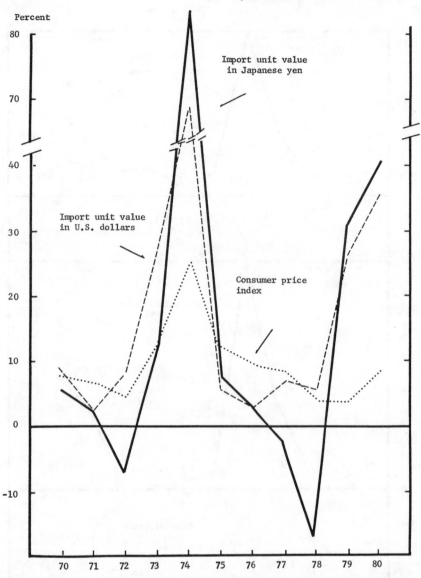

Figure 2-7. Annual Changes in Japanese Import Unit Value in Terms of
U.S. Dollars and Yen and Consumer Price Index, 1970–1980

A sharp rise in import costs and large terms of trade losses affected the
growth of real domestic demand in several ways. Real personal consumption was reduced by the loss in real income, and the growth of real government expenditures, unless offset by discrete fiscal actions, was also affected

by the increased cost of goods and services. Business firms were squeezed by both diminished product demand and increased production costs, the latter for labor, intermediate inputs, and borrowed capital. Nominal interest rates tended to rise because of the diminished money supply in real terms and an increased need for working capital to meet the higher input costs. The situation was made worse by the pursuit of restrictive monetary policy in both countries to dampen the excess demand conditions that existed before the oil shock.

In both Japan and, to a lesser extent, the United States, the money supply in real terms declined sharply in 1974 and 1975. The tightening in liquidity condition exacerbated the deflationary impact of losses in terms of trade, depressing the growth of domestic demand in real terms. For both the United States and Japan, the 1974–1975 decline in real domestic demand far exceeded the direct loss in real income attributable to terms of trade losses. In the United States real domestic demand declined by 1.5 percent for two years following an average annual growth of 4.6 percent in the preceding three years. In Japan it declined by 2.5 percent in 1974 and increased little in 1975, after an average annual growth of nearly 8 percent from 1970 to 1973. (See table 3–2 and figure 3–1.)

Of the major components of domestic demand, the most seriously affected was the interest-rate-sensitive housing industry. In the United States, gross private, residential fixed investment declined by nearly 23 percent in 1974 and more than 12 percent in 1975 after a small drop in 1973. In Japan, where there was a real estate boom fueled by former Premier Tanaka's Program for Restructuring the Japanese Archipelago, the decline in housing investment was not as severe as in the United States. (See table 3–2 and figures 3–3 and 3–4.)

In contrast, the decline in real personal consumption expenditures (PCE) was relatively mild in both countries. In the United States real PCE declined by 0.6 percent in 1974 and increased by 2.2 percent in 1975, following an average annual growth rate of 4.0 percent in the preceding four years. In Japan it declined by 0.8 percent in 1974 and increased by 4 percent in 1975, from a three-year average growth of more than 8 percent from 1970 to 1973. (See table 3–2 and figures 3–3 and 3–4.) The smaller declines in PCEs stemmed partly from the fact that real wages declined relatively little compared to real output and partly from the counter-cyclical nature of the fiscal system. For the United States real wages in manufacturing declined by 0.5 percent in 1974 but increased by 2.6 percent in 1975, following an annual average increase of 1.5 percent in the preceding three years. In Japan, there was an increase of a mere 1.4 percent in 1974, following an annual average growth rate of 9.5 percent in the preceding three years. In 1975, there was a slight drop (figures 2–8 and 2–9).

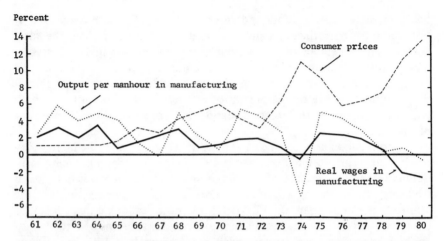

Figure 2-8. Annual Changes in U.S. Consumer Price Index and Output per
Hour and Real Wages in Manufacturing, 1960–1980 (in percent)

The decline or slowdown of housing and private consumption demand,
the deceleration of the growth of world trade, and the tightening of the
financial markets caused business firms to scale down their investment
plans. Summed together for 1974 and 1975, gross private, nonresidential
fixed investment declined by as much as 13 percent in the United States and
by nearly 11 percent in Japan. This was in contrast to an annual average
growth of 6.7 percent in the United States and 5.5 percent in Japan for the
preceding three years. In addition to fixed investment, inventory investment

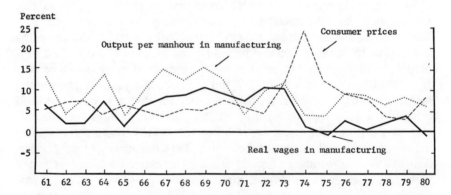

Figure 2-9. Annual Changes in Japanese Consumer Price Index and Output per Hour and Real Wages in Manufacturing, 1960–1980 (in
percent)

was also cut back sharply in both countries because of diminished demand and higher financial costs.

Partially offsetting these declines in domestic demand was an improvement in the real trade balance in 1974 and 1975 caused by a steeper decline in import growth as compared to export growth. Both Japan and the United States were the chief beneficiaries of expanding import demand from the oil exporting countries. Public finance provided another offset to the diminished domestic demand through both discretionary fiscal operations and automatic stabilizers. Because of increased government expenditures and transfers and reduced tax receipts, the fiscal deficit expanded sharply in 1975 in both the United States and Japan, although its increase in 1974 was delayed by the rise in the tax base caused by inflation. As a percentage of GNP, the U.S. deficit expanded from 0.2 percent in 1973 to 0.7 percent in 1974 and 5.1 percent in 1975. In Japan the deficit accentuated the rising trend of the preceding three years, amounting to 3.9 percent in 1974 and 7.4 percent in 1975. (See figures 3-5, 3-6, and 3-7.)

As a result, real output declined by only 0.6 percent in 1974 and 1.1 percent in 1975 in the United States compared to a decline of 1.5 percent each for real domestic demand. For Japan, the counterbalancing effect of improvements in real trade balance and an expanded government deficit was even greater. Together they made it possible for real output to remain or grow two percentage points higher in 1974 and three percentage points higher in 1975 than would otherwise have been the case. (See table 3-2.) However, these counterbalancing forces, while not inconsequential, provided only a partial offset to the sharp declines in real domestic demand that actually occurred in 1974 and 1975.

In conjunction with the decline in real domestic demand, inflation accelerated sharply in both countries but at a higher rate in Japan than in the United States. In Japan the consumer price index rose by 24 percent in 1974 and nearly 12 percent in 1975, while in the United States it increased by about 11 percent and 9 percent during those two years. Japan's much sharper rise in price levels was attributable to its greater reliance on imported fuels, raw materials, and foodstuffs, the depreciation of its currency following the oil shock, the more complete transmission of increased fuel costs, and frenzied speculation by the general public due to fears of global commodity shortages. In comparison, imported oil constituted a much smaller share of domestic demand in the United States (about one-third compared to nine-tenths for Japan), and wellhead prices for crude oil remained under control despite the end of phase IV wage and price controls in April 1974. Although inventory speculation was intense in both Japan and the United States in the months following the oil embargo, fears of commodity shortages were perhaps less widespread in the United States because of its rich natural resource base. In terms of U.S. dollars, Japanese import unit values rose by nearly 70 percent in 1974 compared to 50 percent for the

United States. In yen terms, however, the 1974 rise in Japanese import prices was nearly 84 percent (figure 2-7).

Divergence of Economic Conditions and Price Trends, 1976-1978

Economic conditions diverged widely between the United States and Japan during the three years from 1976 to 1978. In the United States strong recovery in domestic demand and output growth was followed by worsening inflation. In Japan surging inflation was brought under control through prolonged weakness in private domestic demand, increased moderation in wage demands, and a recovery of productivity growth. These differences in economic conditions caused the two countries' bilateral trade balance to move strongly in Japan's favor, thereby intensifying the trade frictions between them.

During 1976 and 1977 the growth of real domestic demand was very brisk in the United States—6 percent per year compared to 4 percent per year in Japan. The recovery in the U.S. economy was led by housing investment and personal consumption expenditures after interest rates dropped sharply in 1975, and spread to nonresidential investment, in particular to energy-related activity. In comparison, the recovery of private consumption and investment demand remained weak in Japan except for a brief rally in housing investment. Even the growth of government expenditures in real terms slowed in 1976 before expanding sharply in 1977-1978. (See figures 3-3 and 3-4.)

Why did private domestic demand remain depressed in Japan much longer than in the United States? Apparently this was not due to any gross inadequacy of fiscal stimuli since Japan's fiscal deficit expanded sharply from 1975 onward to at least twice the size of the U.S. deficit in relation to their respective GNPs. (See figures 3-5, 3-6, and 3-7.) The role played by Japan's monetary policy is more problematic, considering its extreme laxity in 1971-1972 and subsequent reversal to extreme restrictiveness in the aftermath of the first oil shock. Although the monetary policy was held tight longer in Japan than in the United States, steady decline of interest rates did occur in 1976-1977 despite a sharp slowdown in money supply growth. However, the basic reasons must be sought in the sharp decline of corporate profit margins between 1974 and 1976 and a gloomy business outlook. While after-tax profits per unit of output for U.S. nonfinancial, corporate business, in 1972 dollars, recovered quickly in 1976 to rival the 1965-1967 levels, operating profits per unit of sales of Japanese corporate business dropped sharply in 1975 and remained in 1976-1977 barely one-half the average rate of the late 1960s (figure 2-10). The divergent profits situation

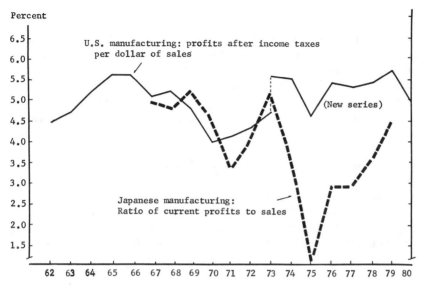

Figure 2-10.   Profit Margins in Manufacturing, 1962–1980

between the two countries resulted from the differential growth in demand and output and differences in the degree of capacity utilization. In 1976–1977 the rate of capacity utilization in the Japanese manufacturing sector was barely 5 to 10 percent higher than the 1975 trough, whereas in the United States it was 12 to 15 percent higher. (See figures 4–5 and 4–6.) Moreover, U.S. businesses appeared to have been quicker in responding to reduced sales volume by adjusting employment levels downward; the adjustment of employment level in Japan was slow and protracted, perhaps reflecting the effect of the lifetime employment system practiced by large corporations. (See figure 4–10.) The different employment practices between the two countries were reflected in contrasting movements between the capacity utilization rate and the unemployment rate. For the United States the two rates exhibited strong contrary movements whereas the Japanese unemployment rate seemed to respond only partially and gradually to changes in the capacity utilization rate. (See figures 4–5 and 4–6.)

Because of differing developments in domestic demand and employment, price trends in the two countries diverged increasingly over time. By 1978, the U.S. economy was vigorously expanding for the third year in a row. The rate of capacity utilization in manufacturing (based on the Federal Reserve series) rose to 84 percent from a trough of 73 percent in 1975, and the civilian unemployment rate declined to 6.0 percent from 8.5 percent in 1975. However, the growth of output per man-hour declined markedly while the rate of increase of unit labor costs accelerated, causing widespread cost-push pressures. (See figure 2–1 and table 4–1.) By contrast, in 1978, the Japanese economy was experiencing the effects of three or four years of business adjustment and consolidation. The index of inventory ratio for finished goods declined from 100 to 82 in 1975. Manufacturing employment continued to decline, while increased production was handled by a recovery in average work hours. (See figure 4–10.) As the rate of capacity utilization gradually recovered, the growth of labor productivity was maintained, and unit labor costs recorded an absolute decline (figures 2–2 and 2–11). As a result, the relative position of unit labor costs again turned sharply in favor of Japan.

Because of the contrasting developments in domestic demand and relative costs, the real trade balance improved strongly for Japan but worsened sharply for the United States. Coupled with the continued deceleration of inflation in Japan and its resurgence in the United States, the yen appreciated sharply against the dollar in 1977–1978. Meanwhile oil prices remained

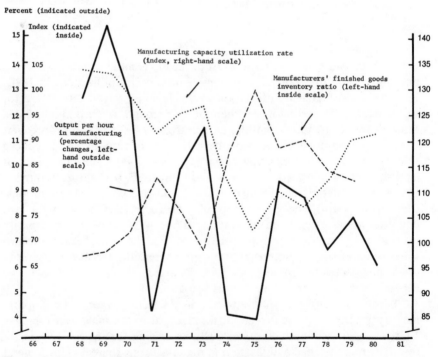

Figure 2–11. Annual Changes in Japan's Manufacturing Output per Hour, Index of Manufacturing Capacity Utilization, and Index of Manufacturers' Finished Goods Inventory Ratio, 1968–1980

stable in the world markets, actually declining in real terms. Because of stable commodity prices and strong yen appreciation, Japanese import unit values in yen terms declined by around 20 percent between 1976 and 1978, while U.S. import values increased by 17 percent. Similarly Japanese export unit values declined, albeit moderately, in yen terms while rising strongly in dollar terms. Thus, the floating exchange rate worked to intensify the divergent price trends and to prolong the imbalance in the current account between the two countries.

Impacts of the Second Oil Shock, 1979–1980

When the second oil shock occurred, Japan and the United States were positioned in vastly different economic situations, a difference that apparently contributed to the subsequent divergence in outcomes. For the United States, the shock exacerbated an already deteriorating domestic cost and price situation. For Japan, however, the shock occurred at a time when the economy was better poised to absorb an external shock; prices were stable after a long process of stabilization and adjustment, and the tempo of economic activity was picking up.

For both countries, the cumulative magnitude of the oil shock was about the same as in 1974. For Japan, import unit values rose by 70 percent in dollar terms and 83 percent in yen terms in 1979–1980, nearly the same magnitude as in 1974. For the United States, they rose by nearly 50 percent in two years, again about the same as in 1974. For Japan, the cumulative loss in terms of trade was greater in 1979–1980 than in 1974 (38 percent versus 25 percent) because of a smaller increase in export unit values. For the United States, however, the loss in terms of trade for 1979–1980 was slightly smaller (14.2 percent versus 15.3 percent) because of a larger rise in export unit values. (See table 2–5 and figures 2–6 and 2–7.)

Despite the similarity in the incidence of the two oil shocks, the outcomes for domestic inflation and output performance have diverged widely between the two countries in the aftermath of the second oil shock. In the United States, there was a worsening in both output and price trends as in the first oil shock. In Japan, however, the slowdown in output growth was much milder while the rate of domestic inflation, as represented by the GNP deflator, continued to decline despite a temporary flare-up of consumer prices.

The divergence between U.S. and Japanese economic performances can be perceived more vividly with the help of a Phillips's curve depicting the evolution of the unemployment rate and annual changes in the GNP deflator, shown in figures 2–11 and 2–12. After hitting a bottom of a 4 percent natural unemployment rate in the latter part of the 1960s, the U.S.

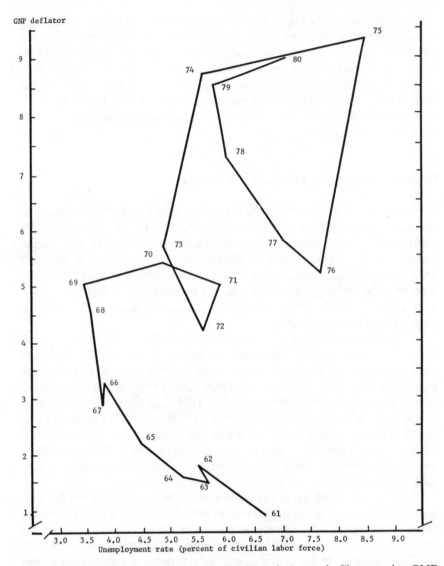

Figure 2-12. U.S. Unemployment Rate and Annual Changes in GNP Deflator, 1961–1980

curve continued to shift outward, despite the wage-price controls of the early 1970s, with each incidence of external price shocks providing a new floor for the unemployment rate and for the rate of increase of the GNP deflator. The Japanese curve, by contrast, is almost perpendicular, with a much narrower range of unemployment rate (ranging from 1.1 to 2.5 percent compared to the U.S. range of 4.0 to 8.5 percent) and a much wider range of inflation rate. Moreover, the Japanese curve does not display a clear trade-off between the unemployment rate and the inflation rate, based on annual data, except for periods such as from 1958 to 1961. On the contrary, there were periods in which the Japanese inflation rate declined in conjunction with a decline in the unemployment rate, such as 1955–1958, 1961–1965, and 1978–1980. In Japan sustained economic expansion in the second half of the 1960s did generate an upward shift in the inflation rate, from the 3.5 to 4.5 percent range in 1962–1964 to the 5 to 7 percent range of 1966–1972. Yet in contrast to the U.S. situation, the disturbances of 1974–1975 were followed by a tendency for the economy to return to price stability despite the second oil shock (figures 2–12 and 2–13).

What caused this divergence in economic performances between the two countries? A key underlying factor has been the divergent developments in labor productivity and unit labor costs. Underlying Japan's successful stabilization efforts after 1975 have been a remarkable moderation of wage behavior and a relatively satisfactory recovery of productivity growth. The resulting stabilization of unit labor costs enabled the business sector to ameliorate the price impact of the sharp rises in the cost of imported fuels and other intermediate inputs. By contrast, in the United States, there was no significant change in wage behavior in the period under review, while the growth of labor productivity deteriorated in 1978–1980 following a recovery in 1975–1977. The resulting upsurge in unit labor costs made it difficult for the business sector to accommodate the sharp rises in the cost of intermediate inputs. (See figures 2–1 and 2–2 and tables 4–1 and 4–2.)

Why was there such a divergence in wage behavior and productivity performance? The moderation of wage behavior in Japan occurred under the circumstance of prolonged sluggishness in the growth of domestic demand relative to the trends prevailed before the first oil shock; important differences in institutions governing employment and labor-management relations underlined the divergent wage and employment behavior between the United States and Japan; and differences in both the employment system and economic structure appeared to have contributed to the divergence in productivity performance.

The contrasting performance of productivity in the aftermath of the second oil shock warrants special attention. In Japan the sustained growth of labor productivity can be attributed partly to a continued rise in the rate of capacity utilization from 1978 onward, while manufacturing employment continued to be adjusted downward. What enabled the rate of capacity utilization to rise, other than the gradual recovery of private domestic demand, was the continued decline in the inventory ratio of finished goods from the peak level of 1975. In comparison with the situation in Japan, the rate of capacity utilization in the United States, while moving contrary to the manufacturers' inventory-shipment ratio, did not always move in line

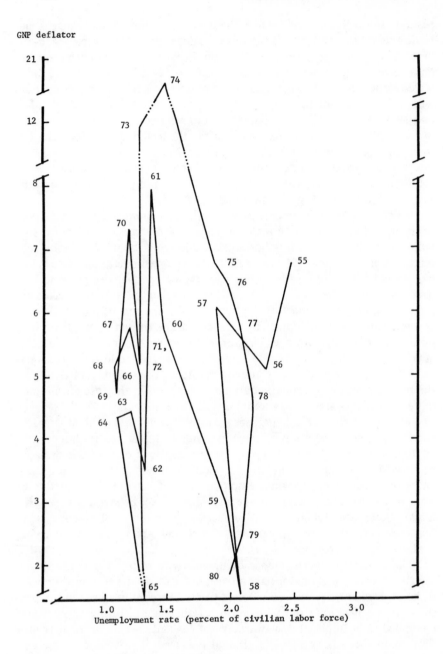

GNP deflator

Figure 2-13. Japanese Unemployment Rate and Annual Changes in GNP
Deflator, 1955-1980

with the growth of output per man-hour. In 1974, for instance, output per man-hour in manufacturing suffered a severe absolute decline while the rate of capacity utilization remained high. Similarly, a sharp decline in the growth of output per man-hour occurred in 1978–1979 when the rate of capacity utilization was at a fairly high level. This end-of-expansion phenomenon in productivity decline, which was not apparent in the Japanese business cycle behavior, appeared to reflect differences in employment practices between the two countries (figures 2–11 and 2–14).

In addition to the decline in labor productivity, the worsening of inflation in the United States during the second oil shock was exacerbated by the coincidental phased decontrol of domestic crude oil prices between June 1979 and January 1981. The Natural Gas Policy Act of 1978, which mandated a gradual decontrol of domestic interstate natural gas prices, also contributed to the general upsurge in the prices of fuels and chemical feedstocks caused by OPEC (Organization of Petroleum Exporting Countries) actions. Since part of the price upsurge in the United States was a delayed response to the global change in the relative price of energy, the cumulative price increases from 1974 to 1980 provided an alternative indicator of price

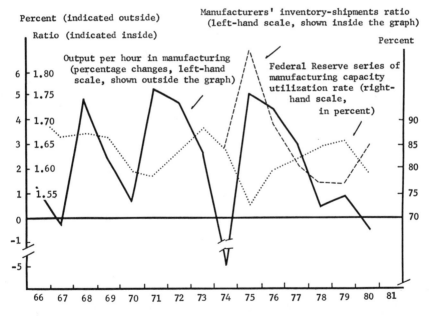

Figure 2–14. Annual Changes in U.S. Manufacturing Output per Hour, Manufacturing Capacity Utilization Rate, and Manufacturers' Inventory-Shipments Ratio, 1966–1980

performance for the entire period. In the seven years from 1974 to 1980, the U.S. consumer price index increased by 85.5 percent, somewhat lower than Japan's 91.5 percent, yet its GNP deflator increased by nearly 68 percent compared to Japan's 53 percent.[12] On this basis, Japan's price performance was better than that of the United States since it managed to have a lower rate of factor cost inflation in spite of a higher rate of consumer price inflation. (See figure 1-1.)

Notes

1. The productivity comparison shown in figure 2-1 is for manufacturing only. A more comprehensive coverage, although not on a per man-hour basis, is given in tables 5-2 and 5-3.

2. Excluding government, private households, the rest of the world, gross housing product of owner-occupied dwellings, and nonprofit institutions.

3. Wages and salaries of employees plus employer's contributions for social security and private benefit plans. Also includes an estimate of wages, salaries, and supplemental payments for the self-employed.

4. See, for example, William D. Nordhaus, "The Recent Productivity Slowdown," *Brookings Papers on Economic Activity* (3:1972).

5. See Robert W. Bednarzik and Deborah P. Klein, "Labor Force Trends: A Synthesis and Analysis," *Monthly Labor Review* (October 1977), for a summary analysis.

6. Elizabeth Waldman, "Viet Nam War Veterans—Transition to Civilian Life," *Monthly Labor Review* (November 1970).

7. See Masaru Yoshitomi, "The Recent Japanese Economy: The Oil Crisis and the Transition to Medium Growth Path," *Developing Economies* 14 (1976):4.

8. On other contributing factors to trend acceleration in Japan's economic growth rate, see Kazushi Ohkawa and Henry Rosovsky, *Japanese Economic Growth: Trend Acceleration in the Twentieth Century* (Stanford: Stanford University Press, 1973), esp. chap. 8.

9. See Otto Eckstein, *The Great Recession* (Amsterdam: North-Holland, 1978), p. 58. However, because price controls caused industrial bottlenecks, prices would have been lower in 1974 had there been no controls in the preceding years.

10. Based on estimate using IMF's multiple exchange rate model.

11. During the same period the IMF index of market prices of thirty-six nonoil primary commodities (excluding petroleum, gold, silver, diamond, coal, phosphate, tobacco, fish and shrimp) rose nearly 76 percent in terms of U.S. dollars.

12. Based on another index, the cumulative increase in Japan's GNP deflator was nearly 60 percent.

3

Macropolicy Responses and the Evolution of Domestic Demand

The oil price shocks caused both cost-push movements and deflationary impacts on domestic demand, confronting the national authorities of oil importing countries with a difficult policy management problem: how to resolve the policy conflict between price stabilization and sustain economic growth. If the authorities were to tighten monetary policy in order to contain cost-push movements, the deflationary impacts on domestic demand would have been exacerbated, further depressing the economy. But if they followed an easy monetary policy in order to ameliorate the deflationary impacts of the terms of trade loss, inflation might have spiraled, in the end requiring an even tighter monetary policy with a stronger depressive effect on the economy. Such a policy dilemma does not exist in a situation where inflation originates from excess demand. In that case, the tightening of monetary policy is both effective and necessary because of its restraining effect on both demand and prices. This, however, is not the case where the price impulses originate from a supply price shock. Under the circumstance, a neutral monetary stance is called for in order not to exacerbate either the inflationary or deflationary impact of the external price shock.

This was not what happened in 1973-1974. Because of the coincidence of the oil price shock with severe excess demand conditions and strong price expectations, most authorities in the industrial countries pursued stringent monetary policies, thereby exacerbating the deflationary impacts of the huge terms of trade loss. Despite the deep recession and severe unemployment that ensued, few countries succeeded in restoring both domestic price stability and a satisfactory economic growth. Even Japan, which is one of few countries that succeeded in restoring domestic price stability, such success was accompanied by a protracted stagnation of private domestic demand. Even worse, many countries have suffered a very severe drop in domestic demand and output growth without restoring the pattern of domestic price stability that existed in the 1960s. (See table 1-1).

Why is it that the depression of domestic demand after the first oil shock led to the restoration of domestic price stability in certain countries (like Japan) but not in many others? Was this due to differences in the severity of demand depression, or was it attributable also to differences in wage and productivity behavior (table 3-1)? Was there a direct link between the severity of demand depression and the significance of wage moderation, or was the difference in the degree of wage moderation attributable

Table 3-1
Growth of Real Domestic Demand, Changes in Terms of Trade and Unit Labor Costs in Manufacturing, and Changes in the Ratio of Factor Cost Inflation to Consumer Price Inflation, for Major Industrial Countries, 1973–1980 over 1963–1973
(annual percentage changes or ratios)

	Real Domestic Demand			Terms of Trade		Unit Labor Costs in Manufacturing			Ratio of Changes in GNP Deflator to Changes in CPI		
	1963–1973	1973–1980	(2)/(1)	1974	1973–1980	1960–1973	1973–1980	(7)/(6)	1962–1972	1973–1980	1978–1980
	(1)	(2)	(3)	(4)	(5)	(6)	(7)	(8)	(9)	(10)	(11)
United Kingdom	3.3	0.2	0.06	−11.5	0.1	8.7	19.1	2.20	1.04	1.01	1.07
Japan	10.6	3.4	.32	−25.4	−7.5	14.6	10.5	.72	.89	.65	.48
United States	4.1	2.0	.49	−15.3	−5.6	5.0	9.3	1.86	1.09	.89	.85
Germany, Federal Republic of	4.4	2.4	.55	−8.0	−2.1	9.4	9.7	1.03	1.29	.99	.94
France	5.6	2.7	.48	−7.1	−2.0	9.4	15.2	1.62	1.07	.98	.91
Italy	4.5	2.5	.56	−25.0	−2.9	12.3	20.1	1.63	1.18	1.04	1.00

Sources: International Monetary Fund, *International Financial Statistics* (various issues) and *World Economic Outlook* (June 1981).

also to differences in institutional factors, such as labor-management relations, unionism, and social security insurance?

Why is it that investment demand was so depressed in Japan compared to the situation before the first oil shock? Is this in fact inevitable, considering the huge loss in terms of trade Japan suffered, or is it partially attributable to the stringent monetary policy pursued by the government? How did fiscal policy evolve in Japan and the United States? Why was fiscal policy not able to offset the depression in domestic demand caused by the loss in terms of trade and restrictive monetary policy?

Was there any major change in national policy responses between the first and the second oil shock? Was the divergence in price trends between the United States and Japan after the second oil shock directly attributable to differences in fiscal and monetary policies, or was it attributable mainly to differences in the underlying economic conditions, particularly with regard to wage behavior and productivity performance? These questions are considered in the discussion of the macropolicy responses to the two oil shocks.

Monetary Policy and the Evolution of Domestic Demand after the First Oil Shock

By many indications, the recovery of domestic demand after the first oil shock took much longer in Japan than in the United States. After suffering an absolute decline of 2.5 percent in 1974, the growth of real domestic demand remained at the 2 to 4 percent range for the next three years, and it was not until 1978 that the 1971–1973 average rate of over 7 percent per year was regained. In comparison, real domestic demand in the United States surged vigorously at around 6 percent per year in both 1976 and 1977 compared to a negative growth of 1.5 percent in the previous two years and an average growth rate of 4.6 percent per year in 1971–1973 (table 3-2 and figure 3-1).

What caused this delay in the recovery of domestic demand in Japan? There were at least three reasons. In terms of the rise in import costs and the loss in terms of trade, the impacts of the oil shock were much harsher for Japan than for the United States. Monetary restraints were also applied longer. Finally, the change in business outlook, both domestically and externally, was far worse for Japan.

Terms of Trade Losses from First Oil Shock

The cumulative loss in Japanese terms of trade from 1974 to 1976 amounted to 35 percent. In comparison, the U.S. loss was 17 percent in 1974 but only

Table 3-2
Growth of Real Domestic Demand and Real Output, 1965-1980
(annual percentage changes)

	Real Domestic Demand[a] (1)	Real GNP (2)	(1) Minus (2) (3)	Personal Consumption Expenditures (4)	Gross Private Domestic Fixed Investment (5)	Of Which: Residential Investment (6)
United States[b]						
1965-1969	4.2	3.9	.3	4.1	3.2	
1969-1973	3.2	3.4	−.2	4.0	4.9	8.4
1973-1974	−1.6	−.6	−1.0	−.6	−8.2	−22.6
1974-1975	−1.5	−1.1	−.4	2.2	−12.2	−12.4
1975-1978	5.5	5.2	.3	5.1	10.2	14.2
1978-1980	.6	1.5	−.9	1.7	2.0	12.0
Japan[b]						
1965-1970	11.3	11.0	.3	8.9	19.5	14.7
1970-1973	7.9	6.7	1.2	8.2	7.5	13.0
1973-1974	−2.5	−.2	−2.3	−.7	−7.4	−12.7
1974-1975	.3	3.6	−3.3	4.1	−3.2	2.5
1975-1978	4.7	5.2	−.5	4.0	4.0	5.7
1978-1980	3.5	5.1	−1.6	3.2	4.8	−5.3

Sources: United States: Council of Economic Advisers, *Economic Report of the President* (February 1982). Japan: Economic Planning Agency: *Keizai Yoran* (Economic data handbook) (1981).

[a]Final consumption expenditures plus gross domestic capital formation.

[b]In 1972 prices for the United States and in 1975 prices for Japan.

12.4 percent when the gain in 1975-1976 is included. The much larger loss in Japan's terms of trade was attributable to a greater reliance on imports of oil, raw materials, and foodstuffs. Moreover, because foreign trade accounted for a larger share of economic activity in Japan than in the United States (11 percent versus 7 percent in 1972-1973 for exports of goods and services as a ratio to GNP), the impact on economic activity of the terms of trade loss was much more severe in Japan. For Japan, the loss in terms of trade (based on export volume in the preceding year) was equivalent to 2.0 percent of GNP in 1974, but the average was 1.0 percent from 1974 to 1976. For the United States, the corresponding losses were 1.1 percent and 0.2 percent, respectively (table 2-5).

These losses in terms of trade, although great, were but a fraction of the actual loss in real output and income suffered by both Japan and the United States during those years when compared to the average growth rates attained by both countries in the pre-oil shock decade. Therefore, the real culprit responsible for the severe demand depression that occurred in both countries was not the loss of terms of trade but demand management policy, which not only failed to offset the deflationary impact of the terms of trade loss but actually exacerbated it.

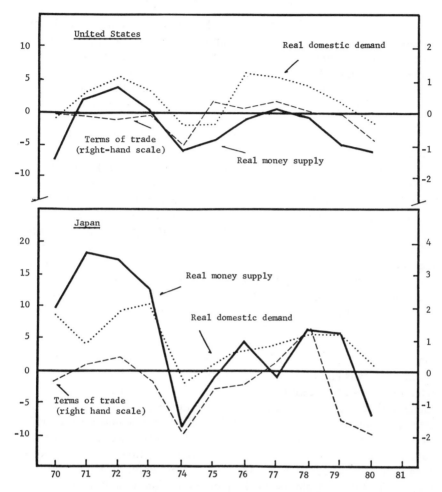

Figure 3-1. Annual Changes in Terms of Trade (in GNP Equivalents), Real Money Supply (Adjusted by Changes in Consumer Price Index), and Real Domestic Demand, 1970–1980 (percentages)

Application of Monetary Brake

In both countries the application of a monetary brake was started well before the onset of the first oil shock as a response to strong upsurges in prices and price expectations. For both countries the acceleration of inflation in 1973 was largely of domestic origin, resulting from an excess demand condition caused by the stimulative policies of the preceding two years. Nevertheless, it was exacerbated by an accelerating rise in foreign trade prices caused by synchronized economic booms among many countries and supply shortages in certain primary commodities. However, following the quantum jump of oil prices in late 1973 and the subsequent worsening of the trade balance, monetary authorities in both countries not only failed to lift the monetary brake to offset the deflationary impact of the current account shift but actually intensified the brake in order to restrain the cost-push effect of the oil price hikes.

In the United States the Federal Reserve system's Open Market Committee called in December 1972 for a "slower growth of monetary aggregates over the months ahead," while raising the federal funds rate, the price for borrowing the excess reserves kept at the Federal Reserve. This policy was maintained through 1973 and 1974 except for an interval during the fourth quarter of 1973.[1] During this period, the federal funds rate was raised from 5.1 percent in November 1972 to 10.8 percent in September 1973 and then to a peak rate of 12.9 percent in July 1974. In consequence, the growth of M1, which averaged 7.0 percent per year in the preceding three years, declined sharply to 4.5 percent each in both 1974 and 1975. Moreover, in real terms, as deflated by changes in the consumer price index, the money supply actually suffered a sharp absolute decline of 5.9 percent in 1974 and 4.3 percent in 1975.

An equally restrictive monetary policy was implemented in Japan during this period. The Bank of Japan began raising its main discount rate (for commercial bills and loans secured by government securities) in April 1973, from the low 4.25 percent that had been in force since mid-1972, and eventually pushed it up to a peak of 9.0 percent in December 1973. Meanwhile, reserve requirements for bank deposits, relatively unchanged since 1965, were raised across the board, and loan controls exercised by the Bank of Japan were extended from city banks to other financial institutions.[2] Because of this so-called overloan situation, the Bank of Japan had been very successful in regulating bank credit expansion as well as the interest rate movements in the money and credit markets. The measures of 1973-1974 proved no exception, perhaps as a result of an overexpansion in the preceding two years.

Moreover, as judged by the movements of key interest rates, the tight money policy was maintained much longer in Japan than in the United States. The U.S. funds rate started declining in the last quarter of 1974 and dropped to an initial trough of 5.2 percent in March 1975. In contrast, the Bank of Japan's peak discount rate was maintained throughout 1974 and the first quarter of 1975. Only after April 1975 was the Japanese discount rate reduced to 8.5 percent, remaining above 6 percent throughout 1975 and 1976 (figure 3-2).

As a result, Japanese monetary growth decelerated even more sharply than did that of the United States. From an annual growth rate of 22.1 per-

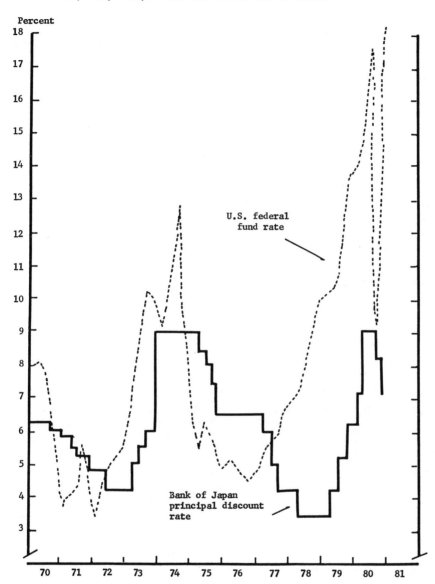

Figure 3–2. Evolution of Key Interest Rates in the United States and Japan, 1970–1980

cent to 26.1 percent in 1971–1973, the growth of M1 in Japan slowed to 13.2 percent in 1974 and 10.3 percent in 1975. Thus, the average annual monetary growth in 1974–1975 amounted to less than one-half of the average rate in the preceding three years, while the comparative ratio for the

United States was about three-fifths. Deflated by changes in the consumer price index, the Japanese money supply declined by 8.9 percent in 1974 and by another 1.4 percent in 1975, compared to an annual average growth of over 16 percent in 1971–1973.

Why did the Japanese authorities pursue a restrictive monetary policy with a vengeance? In 1973 and 1974 Japan was experiencing a much stronger surge in inflation than was the United States. In those two years Japanese import unit values jumped by 106 percent—cushioned by the appreciation of the yen in 1973 but exacerbated by its depreciation in the following year—compared to a cumulative rise of some 79 percent in the United States. Meanwhile, the Japanese consumer price index, stimulated by the rapid expansion of the money supply in 1971–1973, sharply rising import prices, and widespread speculation, jumped by 11.8 percent in 1973 and 24.3 percent in 1974, following an annual increase of only 4 to 7 percent in the preceding three years. By comparison, the acceleration of consumer price inflation in the United States reflected the effect of wage and price controls imposed in 1971 and so was relatively modest, being 6.3 percent in 1973 and 10.9 percent in 1974 compared to an annual increase of 3 to 6 percent in 1970–1972.

Changes in Business Outlook

For the Japanese business sector, which is heavily dependent on external fuels supply and export demand, the events of 1974–1975, following the forced revaluation of its currency in 1971–1973, represented a basic worsening of the external environment. It signified the end of an era based on cheap fuels and raw materials and expanding export markets supported by the Bretton Woods system of fixed exchange rates. These changes were imposed on an economy that after two decades of unprecedented rapid growth experienced with increasing intensity a tightening of the labor markets, shortages of social overhead capital, and social awareness of the environment. These changes indicated that rapid growth in the future would be less certain and would be based more on domestic demand, requiring energy-saving innovations and larger investments for social overhead capital.

The lowering of business expectations in Japan was fueled further by the prolonged stagnation of consumer demand, which increased by only 2.9 percent per year from 1974 to 1976 compared to 7.8 percent per year from 1971 to 1973, the existence of large excess capacities in many industries, and the government's stringent monetary policy. Dampened business expectations were corroborated by the downward adjustment of the economic growth target set by the Japanese government for the second half of the 1970s. Prepared during the gloomy times of the first oil shock, the plan en-

visaged that economic growth would be at slightly over 6 percent per year
compared to the 9.4 percent rate set by the Tanaka cabinet at the beginning
of 1973, a booming year.[3] Under the circumstances, private investment in
plants and equipment, following a cumulative decline of 11.8 percent in real
terms in 1974–1975, remained depressed through 1976–1977 (table 3-2 and
figure 3-3).

In the United States, the 1974–1975 decline in gross private nonresidential investment was equally steep (13.6 percent in real terms for the two
years), although it had a much faster recovery than in Japan. In 1976,
however, it increased by 5.3 percent and continued to expand vigorously at
an average rate of 10.5 percent for the next two years. This resurgence of
U.S. investment in productive capacities was accompanied by a strong
recovery in both housing investment and personal consumption. Particularly strong was the recovery in housing investment, which expanded by
nearly 20 percent (in real terms) for two years, thus fully offsetting the 32
percent loss suffered in the previous two years. Real personal consumption
also increased at a rate of 5.3 percent per year, exceeding even the average
annual rate of 4.6 percent in 1971–1973 (table 3-2 and figure 3-4).

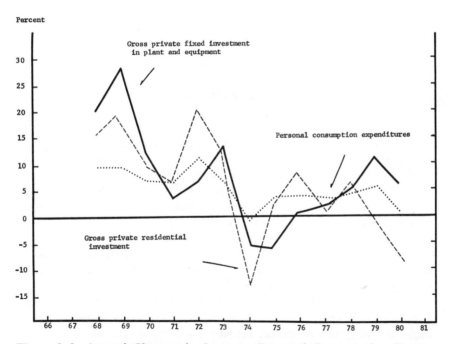

Figure 3-3. Annual Changes in Japanese Personal Consumption Expenditures, Gross Private Fixed Investment in Plant and Equipment, and Gross Private Residential Investment, 1968–1980

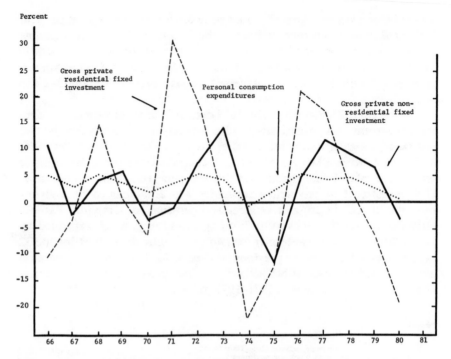

Figure 3-4. Annual Changes in U.S. Personal Consumption Expenditures, Gross Private Nonresidential Fixed Investment, and Gross Private Residential Fixed Investment, 1966–1980

The relatively quick and widespread recovery of economic activity in the United States reflected the general public's return to a business-as-usual psychology following a brief panic at the gas lines. Several factors may have contributed to the endurance of this psychology. Most important was the vastness of the U.S. economy with its rich endowment of natural resources, large and sophisticated industrial base, and highly productive agriculture. Although dependence on imported oil supply had increased rapidly during the late 1960s and early 1970s, this was caused less by actual exhaustion of domestic oil reserves than by a progressive relative cheapening of foreign oil and a public unconvinced of the oil companies' inability to prevent the restructuring of world oil prices.[4] This suspicion was abetted by the inconsistency of U.S. energy policy, which, while giving a false hope of rapidly attaining energy independence, actually discouraged earnest conservation efforts through the continued control of wellhead prices of domestically produced crude, in addition to causing increased oil imports through measures to equalize crude oil costs for domestic refiners. Despite the delay in a restructuring of the price of domestic oil, however, industrial activity related to oil exploration picked up sharply.

Evolution of Fiscal Policy and Its Limitations

While monetary policy was assigned the role of containing inflation in both countries, fiscal policy was charged with the task of supporting domestic demand. This combination turned out to be unsuccessful for several reasons. First, under rapidly rising inflation, tax revenues tended to increase rapidly because of progressive income tax systems in both countries, thus weakening the fiscal system's function as an automatic stabilizer. This happened in both countries, particularly during 1974 when each country's tax revenues, as a percentage of GNP, increased significantly despite a sharp decline in real output. Second, discretionary fiscal actions tended to be enacted and implemented with considerable delay, thus failing to provide support for domestic demand just when the impact of terms of trade losses and monetary restraint was most severe. This was true for both countries in 1974. Third, due to inevitable mismatches between the components of private and public expenditures, expansion in fiscal spending could only partially offset losses in the growth of private domestic demand and exports. In consequence, despite the rapid expansion of fiscal expenditures as a percentage of GNP in Japan, excess capacity remained substantial several years after the first oil shock in industries heavily dependent on private domestic demand or exports.

In the United States the federal deficit, on a calendar year basis, increased only to 0.8 percent of GNP in 1974, up from 0.4 percent in 1973, but in 1975 it expanded sharply to 4.5 percent before tapering off gradually in the following three years. In Japan the central government's deficit, on a fiscal year basis, also grew slowly at first, from a surplus 0.2 percent of GNP in 1973 to a deficit 0.6 percent in 1974, but it expanded sharply to 3.0 percent in 1975. However, while tapering off occurred in the United States after 1975, the Japanese budgetary deficit continued to expand through the following four years, reaching a peak of over 6 percent of GNP in 1979. By 1975, the U.S. federal deficit had declined to only 0.6 percent of GNP, but it expanded again to 2.4 percent in 1980 as a result of a new recession (figure 3-5).

In both countries the expansion of the fiscal deficit was caused by an initial decline and subsequent stagnation of the growth of budgetary receipts under recessionary conditions and by increased government expenditures for social security and other transfers for countercyclical purposes. Direct purchases of goods and services, as a percentage of GNP, fluctuated in Japan during 1975–1976 and increased in 1977–1979 but declined in the United States from 1976 through 1979 (figures 3-6 and 3-7).

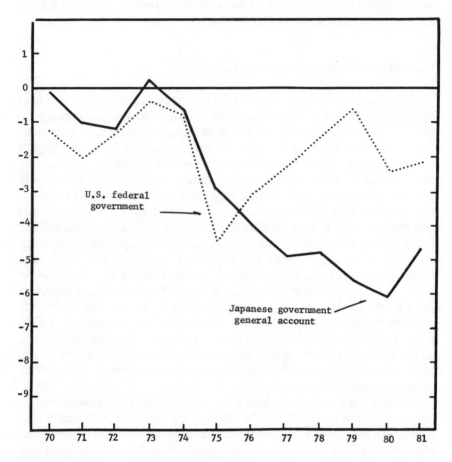

Figure 3-5. Budget Deficit in Relation to GNP, 1970–1981 (percentages)

Both the U.S. and Japanese central government receipts, as a percentage of GNP, increased in 1974 because of the impact of inflation on the income tax base despite a sharp decline in the growth of the economy. In the following year, U.S. receipts, helped by legislation for a 10 percent tax rebate in 1974 and tax cuts for both individuals and corporations in 1975, declined by 1.6 percentage points of GNP.[5] Japan's receipts also declined in 1975, by as much as 2.5 percentage points of GNP. In the ensuing years U.S. receipts, as a percentage of GNP, rapidly recovered until they returned to the level of 1974, partly because of expansion in social security payroll taxes. Japanese receipts, in contrast, remained stagnant relative to GNP because of the depressed state of the tax base.

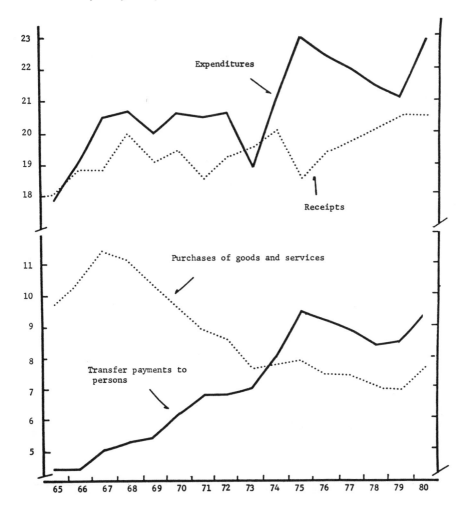

Figure 3-6. Evolution of U.S. Federal Government Receipts and Expenditures in Relation to GNP, 1965-1980 (percentages)

On the expenditures side, the pattern of change was even more different between the two countries. U.S. federal expenditures, reflecting cyclical movements in transfers to individuals and states, expanded by 2.1 percentage points of GNP in 1975 but declined gradually over the next four years. Japanese expenditures, which had begun to expand in the early 1970s, were static initially but expanded from 1976 to 1980. Expressed as a percentage of GNP, U.S. federal expenditures in 1980 were 22.9 percent, or only 2.5 percentage points higher than in 1969-1970, but Japanese expenditures for

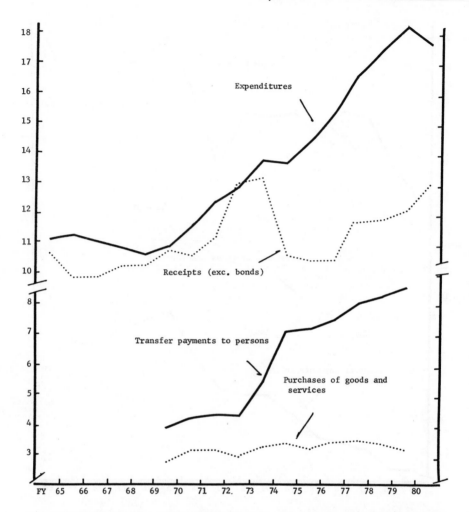

Figure 3-7. Evolution of Japanese Central Government Receipts and Expenditures in Relation to GNP, FY 1965–1981 (percentages)

1980 were 6.5 percentage points higher than at the beginning of the 1970s. From a level roughly one-half of U.S. expenditures, Japanese expenditures grew to three-quarters of the U.S. level within a decade. Until 1975 this growth was attributable to the expansion of both social security transfers and direct government purchases of goods and services and since 1975 to the continued expansion of social security payments.

Nevertheless, in real terms, the Japanese government's purchases of goods and services (for both consumption and capital formation) increased by only 2.8 percent per year during 1974–1976 compared to 6.8 percent per year in the preceding three years. Such a low rate of real growth apparently was inadequate to offset the sharp slump that occurred in private domestic demand. In addition, because of the mismatches between the components of private domestic demand and public outlays, excess capacities remained serious in many industrial sectors, such as steel, nonferrous metals, chemicals, and cement. In 1977, the rate of capacity utilization in all manufacturing industries (excluding shipbuilding) had returned only to 84 percent of the level in 1973, but the rate was even lower in the specific industries. (See figures 4–6 and 5–4.)

Because of the failure of fiscal policy to offset fully the decline in the growth of private domestic demand and exports, the growth of real domestic demand remained sluggish in Japan during 1976–1977, a time of strong recovery in the United States. This divergence in cyclical position, combined with the sharp depreciation of the yen-dollar rate that occurred after the first oil shock, caused a strong expansion of Japanese exports to the United States. During those two years Japanese export volume expanded by more than 15 percent per year while its import volume grew by only 5.5 percent per year. U.S. export volume increased by less than 2 percent per year, while imports jumped by 16 percent per year (figure 3–8). As a consequence, Japan's current account moved from a deficit of $5 billion in 1974–1975 to a surplus of $15 billion in 1976–1977, while the U.S. current account turned from a strong surplus position in 1974–1976 to an $11 billion deficit in 1977 (figures 3–9 and 3–10). This led to strong pressure from the United States and international financial institutions urging Japan—and West Germany—to expand domestic demand in order to lead the world economy out of the protracted slump.[6] Subsequently Japan's government expenditures expanded, by 9 percent in 1977 and 10 percent in 1978. This expansion was coupled with the turnaround of the yen-dollar rate from the fourth quarter of 1976 and caused Japan's real trade balance to worsen over time. However, because of the so-called J curve effect caused by the sharp appreciation of the yen, Japanese current account surplus continued to expand, reaching $18 billion in 1978 (figure 3–9). The U.S. current account deficit also remained at the same high level as in 1977 because of the J curve effect and a sharp increase in oil imports.

The incident demonstrated the difficulty, even under a flexible exchange rate system, of a major country's following an independent demand management policy without considering its external impacts. While the evidence indicated that the expansion of countercyclical expenditures by the Japanese government was too late and not enough to prevent the disequilibrium in its bilateral trade balance with the United States from developing into an international crisis, it also showed that the particular policy mix followed by Japan, the United States, and many other industrial

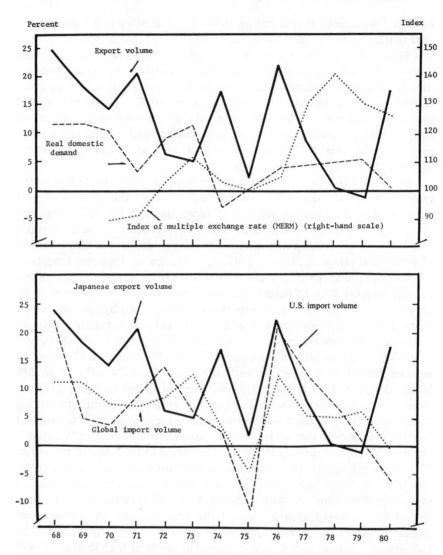

Figure 3-8. Changes in Japanese Export Volume and Selected Variables, 1968-1980

countries in countering the inflationary and deflationary impacts of the oil shock was flawed. This policy mix—using monetary policy to restrain the impact on price inflation and fiscal policy to offset deflationary impacts—was ineffective in attaining its objectives under the circumstances of oil price shocks.

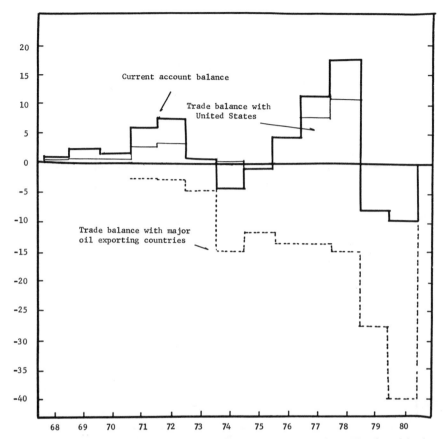

Figure 3-9. Japan's Balances on Current Account and on Trade with the United States and Major Oil Exporting Countries, 1968–1980 (billion U.S. dollars)

Stringent monetary policy proved that it could exacerbate the deflationary impact of losses in terms of trade, while discretionary fiscal actions, for various reasons, turned out to be inadequate to offset the deflationary impacts of terms of trade losses and tight monetary policy. Partly because of the mismatches in private and public expenditures, the Japanese government was required to maintain the expansion of fiscal expenditures at a high level for a prolonged period of time without fully reviving domestic demand. Such large-scale expansion in the fiscal deficits was not without problems, as the U.S. experience indicated and as the Japanese authorities have begun to find out.

It is also debatable whether the tight monetary policy has been chiefly responsible for the ultimate success of price stabilization in Japan. Without

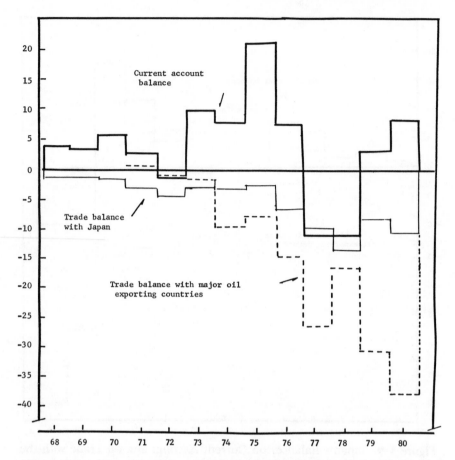

Figure 3-10. U.S. Balances on Current Account and on Trade with Japan
and Major Oil Exporting Countries, 1968–1980 (billion U.S.
dollars)

restraining the rise of real wages and consequently of unit labor costs, it
would have been difficult to contain the price impact of the quantum jumps
in oil prices. This has been the basic difference in price stabilization experiences between Japan and the United States in the period under review.

Although wage behavior and productivity trends in the two countries
are examined in detail in the next two chapters, it may be appropriate to
suggest here that the burdens on monetary policy to perform as an anti-
inflationary tool and on fiscal policy to perform as a countercyclical tool
can be lessened to the extent that closer labor-management cooperation are
promoted. Such cooperation should help to reduce violent fluctuations in

monetary growth while keeping the growth of fiscal expenditures more directly related to the nation's social and economic needs rather than substituting for cyclical changes in private demand. For countercyclical purposes, it apears that a strengthening of automatic stabilization mechanisms through social security and other income transfers, as well as discretionary tax actions, may prove more effective.

Policy Responses to the Second Oil Shock

The second oil shock that occurred at the end of 1978 caused both the United States and Japan losses in terms of trade and jumps in import unit values, which, for 1979 and 1980 together, were cumulatively of roughly the same magnitude as that which had occurred in 1973–1974. How did the authorities of both countries react to the inflationary and deflationary impacts of the second oil shock? Did they learn any lessons from their experiences in the aftermath of the first oil shock? Or did they largely repeat the same response pattern, using monetary policy to restrain the inflationary impact of the oil price hike and fiscal policy to offset the deflationary impacts of terms of trade losses and restrictive monetary policies?

In the United States, monetary policy continued to be used as the main tool for controlling inflation. However, since October 1979 the FOMC (Federal Open Market Committee) has altered its technique of monetary control, substituting the volume of bank reserves for interest rates as the day-to-day guide in conducting open market operations. Previously the basic approach employed by the Federal Reserve system was to supply or to absorb bank reserves through open market operations for the purpose of holding the key federal funds rate within a relatively narrow but changing band thought to be consistent with desired growth of the money stock. This shift was considered desirable because under conditions of heightened inflationary expectations, it was not easy for the Federal Reserve to predict correctly the public's desired money holdings at given levels of nominal interest rates.[7] Under the new approach, the Open Market Desk focused on attaining a given level of nonborrowed reserves through its daily open market operations and although the relationship between bank reserves and the money stock—the so-called reserve multiplier—was variable, the FOMC could adjust the path for nonborrowed reserves to attain the necessary results for monetary growth.[8]

Under the new approach, interest rates in the money markets became extremely volatile as the key federal funds rate was let loose. The latter jumped initially in October 1979 to nearly 16 percent, from the 10 to 12 percent range that had prevailed during the early part of the year, but it later fell to the 13 to 14 percent range from November 1979 to January 1980. It then took off again in March and reached 19.5 percent, came down steeply to below 9 percent by the middle of the year, and scaled a new high of nearly 20 percent in the last quarter (figure 3–2). Both the prime lending rates of the major banks and short-term Treasury bill rates followed suit in fluctuating wildly, the former above and the latter below the federal funds rate. The growth of the money stock, particularly M1A and M1B, also fluctuated wildly and was substantially below the target zone during the first quarter of 1980 before moving up sharply during the second half of the year.[9]

In the process of this experiment, real economic activity suffered a severe decline in the first half of 1980 before recovering in the second half. For the year as a whole, real GNP declined by 0.2 percent following a gain of 3.2 percent in 1979. Yet inflation continued to accelerate, with the consumer price index rising by 13.5 percent, following an increase of 11.3 percent in the preceding year, and the GNP deflator rising by 9.0 percent, or a half percentage point higher than in 1979. As in 1973–1974 the consumer price index rose faster than the GNP deflator because of the inclusion of sharply rising costs of food, energy, and interest on mortgages for housing.

The extraordinarily high interest costs discouraged the growth of private consumption and investment expenditures, which were already suffering from a loss in real purchasing power caused by rising inflation. Most severely affected were the interest-rate-sensitive automobile industry and residential construction. During the second quarter of 1980, sales of domestic cars fell to an annual rate of 5.5 million units, lower than the rate at the depth of the 1974–1975 recession. Total private housing starts, which had declined since fall 1979, hit a near record postwar low in May 1980 after mortgage rates topped 16 percent in April and some lenders stopped issuing mortgages. As final sales stagnated during 1980, the rate of capacity utilization in manufacturing fell markedly by the second half of the year. The increased margin of unused capacities, sharply declining corporate profits, and steep interest costs discouraged business spending, except in special areas such as oil exploration and energy-related retooling.[10]

While the monetary policy turned restrictive, fiscal operations turned expansionary, although not as much as in 1975, in terms of GNP. For 1980, this was estimated at 2.4 percent compared to 4.5 percent in 1975. In terms of GNP, federal tax receipts did not decline in 1980, as compared to a 1.5 percentage point decline recorded in 1975, while the expansion of fiscal expenditures was less sharp than in 1975. In 1980 as in 1975, the increase in transfer payments played the principal role in stabilizing aggregate expenditures, although the share of federal purchases of goods and services supported by increased defense outlays also expanded (figure 3–6).

In Japan also, monetary policy has remained the main policy tool for fighting inflation. Beginning in April 1979, the Bank of Japan's discount rate, which had been reduced to a postwar low of 3.5 percent since March

1978, was raised step by step until it reached 9.0 percent in March 1980, a peak previously reached in December 1973. This peak rate was maintained until August 1980 when it began to be adjusted slowly downward (figure 3–2). Meanwhile, the Bank of Japan strengthened its window guidance over the banks' credit expansion and raised reserve requirements for bank deposits in March and April 1980. These higher reserve requirements were maintained through November 1980 before they were adjusted downward. As a consequence, interest rates in the money and capital markets rose sharply, and the growth of M1 slowed sharply from 10.8 percent in 1978, to 9.9 percent in 1979 and to a mere 0.8 percent in 1980. Although not as dramatic, the decline in the growth of M2 in 1980 was also substantial.

Meanwhile the government attempted to restrain the continued growth of the fiscal deficit, which had remained at about 5 percent of GNP in 1978. The expansion of the fiscal deficit after 1975 had reached such a proportion that its effectiveness as a countercyclical tool was beginning to be questioned. Concern was expressed that the continued issuance of national debts in large amounts could crowd out private loan demand. Furthermore, excess supply in the bond market was making it difficult for the government to issue more bonds without raising their yields, thereby creating capital losses for holders of earlier issues.

Therefore, starting from fiscal year (FY) 1978, the government attempted to curtail the growth of fiscal expenditures while also introducing selective tax measures, including a tax on petroleum. In addition, selective adjustments were made in tax rates to stimulate investments. More tax measures (including a 25 percent increase in the gasoline tax) were introduced in FY 1979 to boost government revenues, and the contracting rate of public works was slowed down as private sector activity picked up in early 1979. During calendar year (CY) 1979 the growth of government purchases (for both consumption and investment) in real terms slowed to 3.6 percent from 12.7 percent in the preceding year, while the growth of real, private fixed investment accelerated from 6.8 percent to 11.2 percent. Despite these changes, however, neither the ratio of the fiscal deficit to GNP nor the proportion of the deficit financed by bond issues declined until 1980.

As the economy recovered from 1979 through the first half of 1980, tax revenues increased rapidly while fiscal expenditures were sharply cut back. In consequence, the ratio of the general account deficit to GNP declined, by 0.5 percent, to 6.0 percent while the proportion of bond issues to general account expenditures declined from the preceding year's 35.4 percent to 32.7 percent. Although the government planned further cutbacks in the fiscal deficit for FY 1981, the growth of private consumption and investment slowed sharply in the second half of 1980 as the deflationary impact of terms of trade losses caused by the second oil shock and stringent monetary policy began to take its toll.

The Japanese outcomes for price stabilization were vastly different from the situation in the United States. Although both the rate of increase for the wholesale price index and the consumer price index accelerated, cumulative increases for 1979–1980 were much smaller than in 1974–1975. The wholesale price index increased by 26.4 percent in 1979–1980 compared to 35.3 percent in 1974–1975 while the consumer price index rose by 11.9 percent against 39 percent earlier. Most important of all, the composite GNP deflator increased by a mere 3.9 percent for those two years compared to a cumulative increase of over 30 percent in 1974–1975.

The stability of Japan's value-added inflation in the aftermath of the second oil shock was made possible by the stability of unit labor costs in manufacturing, which, following a decline of 2.6 percent in 1978, declined by another 2.9 percent in 1979 and increased by only a mere 0.9 percent in 1980. This was a far cry from the cumulative increase of 66.6 percent in 1973–1975. Underlying stable unit labor costs in 1979–1980 were a continuing moderation in the rise of nominal wages and the maintenance of a satisfactory growth in labor productivity. The former increased by only 14.1 percent in 1979–1980 compared to a cumulative increase of 41 percent in 1974–1975, while the latter increased by 7.0 percent per year in 1979–1980 against a decline of 1.0 percent per year earlier. (See figures 2–1 and 2–2 and table 4–1.)

In contrast, the inflation of U.S. unit labor costs (in manufacturing) accelerated in the aftermath of the second oil shock. From 7.7 percent in 1977, their increase accelerated to 8.2 percent in 1979 and 11.1 percent in 1980. Underlying the worsening labor cost situation were the accelerated increases in wage rates and unsatisfactory productivity. The former increased by 7.4 percent in 1979 and 11.6 percent in 1980, following an increase of 7.3 percent in 1978, whereas the latter increased by a mere 0.6 percent per year in 1978–1979 before suffering an absolute decline of 9.5 percent in 1980. (See figures 2–1 and 2–2 and table 4–1.)

The divergence of progress in price stabilization in the United States and Japan in the aftermath of the second oil shock appears to have derived less from differences in the stance of monetary and fiscal policies than from differences in underlying business conditions and associated trends in wages and productivity. It is true that the quick imposition of a stringent monetary policy in Japan after the second oil shock may have caused a pronouncement effect, which discouraged the repetition of widespread speculative activity as in 1973–1974. However, after years of sluggish growth and a loose labor market situation, Japanese consumers appeared subdued and business operators cautious. Whereas there was a recurrence of speculative activity in the United States in selected commodities, particularly in gold and silver, in the wake of the second oil shock as in the first, it is doubtful whether such speculation would have been repeated in Japan, even without the discouragement of a restrictive monetary policy, considering the divergence in economic conditions between the two countries that had developed since 1976. If so, then the economic cost—in terms of a potential loss in output and employment from the restrictive monetary policy—may have been excessive as it was after the first oil shock.

In the United States also, the loosening of the federal funds rate, in the absence of any major moves toward reducing the growing federal fiscal deficit, may have complicated the outlook for business recovery. Although the liberation of interest rates is to be welcomed because of the hope that they will move procyclically and hence work as an additional built-in stabilizer, this may not have happened when domestic prices accelerated, partly because of exogeneous price shocks and the decontrol of domestic oil and gas prices.[11] Certainly the effect of such a shift in monetary control would have been greater in calmer years like 1976–1977 or a few years after the second oil shock.

This shift may also have had an unintended dampening effect on economic activity in the rest of the world at a time when activity needed to be stimulated to compensate for the cyclical downturn in the United States. Not only is external borrowing by countries with external deficits discouraged, but monetary authorities in other major industrial countries are also compelled to move their key interest rates in line with the movements of their counterparts in the United States in order to discourage excessive capital outflow or inflow. It is doubtful that such interest movements will always coincide with these countries' own domestic economic need and may accentuate the U.S. economy's cyclical impact on the rest of the world.

Notes

1. See, for example, Alan S. Blinder, *Economic Policy and the Great Stagflation* (New York: Academic Press, 1979), pp. 184–187.

2. See, for example, Yoshio Suzuki, *Money and Banking in Contemporary Japan* (New Haven: Yale University Press, 1980), pp. 178–179, and Bank of Japan, *Economic Statistics Annual* (1980), pp. 35–39.

3. Such cautiousness reflected the fact that since 1970 the Japanese government has repeatedly overestimated its growth targets, just as it repeatedly underestimated such targets in the 1950s and the 1960s.

4. For a more detailed treatment of the developments leading to an increased U.S. dependence on imported oil and post-1974 oil market developments, see my "Oil Price, Term of Trade, and Balance of Payments" (unpublished manuscript, 1982), chap. 2.

5. Board of Governors, Federal Reserve System, "The Federal Budget in the 1970s," *Federal Reserve Bulletin* (September 1978):713.

6. See International Monetary Fund, *Annual Report* (1978), p. 30, and Marina v. N. Whitman, "The Locomotive Approach to Sustaining World Recovery: Has It Run Out of Steam?" in American Enterprise Institute, *Contemporary Economic Problems, 1978* (Washington, D.C.: AEI, 1978).

7. During the mid-1960s (1974 to 1976) and again during 1979, the growth of the narrow money stock was much weaker than what was predicted based on past relationships of money to income and interest rates. See Stephen Goldfeld, "The Case of the Missing Money," *Brookings Papers on Economic Activity* (3:1976), and John Wenninger, Lawrence Radecki, and Elizabeth Hammond, "Recent Instability in the Demand for Money," *FRBNY Quarterly Review* (Summer 1981).

8. See Federal Reserve Board, "Monetary Policy Report to Congress," *Federal Reserve Bulletin* (March 1981):202.

9. See Federal Reserve Board of New York, "Monetary Policy and Open Market Operations in 1980," *FRBNY Quarterly Review* (Summer 1981):57. M1A is the narrowest of the money stock measures. M1B is M1A plus interest-bearing checkable deposits at all depositary institutions.

10. See, for example, Mark A. Wasserman and Shirley N. Watt, "The Economy in 1980," *Federal Reserve Bulletin* (January 1981):5–8.

11. See James L. Pierce, "Making Reserve Targets Work," in Federal Reserve Bank of Boston, *Controlling Monetary Aggregates III* (Proceedings of a Conference Held in October 1980), p. 342.

4

Wage-Price Behavior under External Price Shocks and Productivity Slowdown

During the 1960s the moderation of cost inflation in the industrialized countries was facilitated by at least two factors: a declining trend in the prices of raw materials and fuels relative to factor costs and the satisfactory growth of labor productivity relative to steadily rising wage costs. The situation changed drastically in the 1970s in the aftermath of a global commodity boom, quantum jumps in oil prices, and the deep recession and sluggish economic growth that followed. In consequence, not only was the declining trend in relative material costs reversed, but the previous favorable relation between productivity growth and wage growth deteriorated. The resulting increase in both material costs and unit labor costs changed the basic character of inflation from that of primarily demand-pull to primarily cost-push. This change sharply reduced the efficacy of monetary policy as a tool for controlling inflation. Instead policies to promote labor-management collaboration and to reduce unit labor costs became more important. Under the changed circumstances of the 1970s, without the accompaniment of effective policies to stabilize unit labor costs, monetary restraint by itself may not attain the purpose of price stabilization, except at a cost of huge losses in employment and real output. This is exemplified by the contrasting experience in inflation and price stabilization in Japan and the United States in the period since the first oil shock.

In the years that followed the deep recession in 1974–1975, both wage and productivity behavior and underlying economic conditions diverged widely between the United States and Japan. In the United States, a strong recovery in the growth of domestic demand was accompanied by steadily increasing employment and a marked decline in the rate of civilian unemployment. On the other hand, an initial decline in unit labor costs was reversed as a continued rise of nominal wages at high rates was accompanied by a steady decline in the growth of real output per man-hour. By contrast, the growth of domestic demand and employment remained sluggish in Japan until 1978, although the rate of civilian unemployment increased relatively little as compared to the United States. However, unit labor costs continued to experience an absolute decline as a marked deceleration in the growth of nominal wages was accompanied by a steady growth in real output per man hour.

The questions, then, are: Why was there a marked moderation of wage behavior in Japan after 1975 while there was not a similar, distinct change in the United States? Was this difference in wage behavior attributable to the divergent economic conditions that prevailed in the two countries, or was it attributable also to differences in institutional factors, specifically the employment system and unionism? Why did productivity performance, following an initial recovery, deteriorate in the United States despite a strong recovery of domestic demand and capacity utilization, while in Japan the growth of labor productivity held at a satisfactory rate despite a sluggish growth of domestic demand? This chapter is devoted to an analysis of the divergence in wage behavior between the United States and Japan. Major factors underlying the differential trends in productivity are examined in chapter 5.

Policy Approaches to Price Stabilization under External Price Shocks

The need for pursuing effective policies to stabilize unit labor costs under the condition of external price shocks was illustrated in chapter 1 with the aid of figure 1-1. There it is assumed that the supply curve for real output is upward sloping and the aggregate demand curve is downward sloping in a coordinate where the abscissa indicates real output and the ordinate price level. A quantum jump in import prices is assumed to shift both the supply and the demand curves inward. The supply curve shifts because of a rise in the costs of materials, fuels, and wages. The demand curve shifts because of losses in purchasing power caused by the higher cost of living, a rise in the interest rate caused by the increased demand for money in nominal terms but reduced supply of it in real terms, and weakened inventory demand associated with reduced final demand and increased financial cost. To some extent, the inward shift in the demand curve is offset by the automatic stabilizing effect of reduced payments for income taxes (although this part of the effect may be weakened by the increase in tax base caused by the inflation) and increased income transfers under the social security system. The inward shift of the supply curve raises supply cost for a given level of real output, while the inward shift of the demand curve reduces the amount of real output demanded at a given price level. The new equilibrium, say, at point C may have a smaller output (Y_3) with a higher price level (P_3). If the authorities tighten the monetary policy, output may fall further to point Y_4, although the price level may go lower.

To avoid falling into this pit of stagflation, the authorities may take a series of policies and measures whose combined effects are to shift the supply curve back to the right. Such a shift can take place with the aid of a moderation in wage demands, which will increase in response to the rise in the cost of living caused by the higher import costs; a substitution away from imported fuels or other materials whose costs have risen; and an improved productivity performance over time. Moderation of wage demands—tantamount to a cutback in real wages—can take place only if it is in exchange for the maintenance of employment, which otherwise will decline. To this effect, the government can promote labor-management collaboration by means of direct intervention in the wage negotiation process or through granting tax incentives (such as a temporary cutback in payroll taxes) to businesses that otherwise would implement a temporary layoff of workers. Substitution of imported fuels or materials can be promoted through the use of tax incentives, but this may contribute less toward productivity improvements than toward restoring the external balance. Improving productivity under external price shocks is not an easy task, but the government can aid this by using tax incentives to maintain investment demand and capacity utilization. In the short run, the pursuit of restrictive monetary policy in response to an external price shock works against the maintenance of capacity utilization and productivity growth because of its depressive effect on the growth of domestic demand.

Divergence of Trends in the Wage Rate, Unit Labor Costs, and Finished Goods Prices in the United States and Japan since the First Oil Shock

Since the first oil shock, there has been a sharp divegence in wage behavior between the United States and Japan. This divergence is found not only in the movements of wages but also in those of unit labor costs and finished goods prices for manufactures. From 1974 to 1981, hourly compensation for U.S. manufacturing workers increased by 9.8 percent per year in nominal terms, nearly twice the rate (5.0 percent per year) that prevailed in the preceding thirteen years. In comparison, nominal hourly compensation for Japanese manufacturing workers increased by 11.1 percent per year during the same period but at less than three-fifths of the rate that prevailed in the preceding thirteen years. This divergence in wage trends was even more pronounced during the five years after the explosive spurt of 1974–1975. From 1976 to 1981, Japanese hourly compensation increased only 7.1 percent per year against a U.S. rate of 9.4 percent per year. Finally, although the Japanese wage rate trend was down except for a brief resurgence in 1979, the U.S. trend was up except for a moderate decline in 1978 (table 4–1 and figures 4–1 and 4–2).

More important from the view of international competition, the marked deceleration in the growth rate of Japanese wages took place against the background of a relatively small deceleration in the rate of growth of labor productivity. Although quite sharp from the Japanese standpoint, this

Table 4-1
Evolution of Hourly Compensation, Real Output per Man-Hour, and Unit Labor Costs in Manufacturing, 1960–1981
(annual percentage changes)

	Hourly Compensation	Real Output per Man Hour	Unit Labor Costs
United States			
1960–1973	5.0	3.0	1.9
1973–1981	9.8	1.5	8.2
1960–1965	3.6	4.2	–.6
1965–1970	6.0	1.8	7.9
1970–1973	6.2	4.2	1.9
1973–1975	11.2	.2	11.0
1975–1981	9.4	1.9	7.4
Japan			
1960–1973	15.1	10.3	4.4
1973–1981	11.1	6.8	4.0
1960–1965	13.4	8.5	4.5
1965–1970	15.0	13.1	1.7
1970–1973	18.0	8.5	8.8
1973–1975	23.9	3.1	20.2
1975–1981	7.1	7.2	–.1

Sources: Patricia Capdevilelle and Donato Alvarez, "International Comparisons of Trends in Productivity and Labor Costs," *Monthly Labor Review* (December 1981), and other articles on the same subject published in other issues of the same magazine.

deceleration was nevertheless much milder compared to the U.S. productivity slowdown and resulted in a marked gain in relative unit labor costs in Japan's favor. The growth rate of real output per man-hour in U.S. manufacturing industries declined by one-half during the period under review, from 3.0 percent per year in the 1961–1973 period to 1.5 percent per year

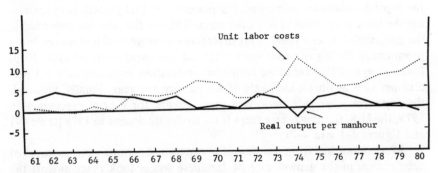

Figure 4-1. U.S. Real Output per Man-Hour and Unit Labor Costs in Manufacturing, 1961–1980 (annual percentage changes)

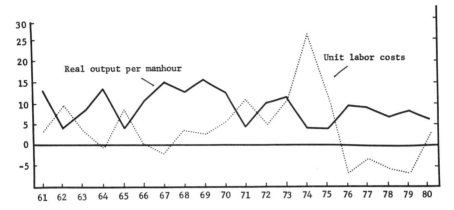

Figure 4-2. Japanese Real Output per Man-Hour and Unit Labor Costs in Manufacturing, 1961–1980 (annual percentage changes)

between 1974 and 1981. Since there was a near doubling of growth in wage levels at 9.8 percent per year, the result was an increase of unit labor costs at 8.2 percent per year in the period after the first oil shock, compared to a mere 1.9 percent per year in the preceding thirteen years. By contrast, the growth rate of Japanese labor productivity in manufacturing declined by only one-third during the same period, from 10.3 percent per year in the 1961–1973 period to 6.8 percent per year between 1974 and 1980. With a slowdown in the growth rate of hourly compensation at 11.1 percent per year, this resulted in a moderate decline in the rate of increase of unit labor costs at 4.0 percent per year in the post-oil shock period, compared to an annual average increase at 4.4 percent in the preceding thirteen years (table 4-1 and figures 4-1 and 4-2).

The sharp divergence in movements of unit labor costs, given a similar rate of increase in the prices of material inputs (8.1 percent per year for Japan and 8.4 percent per year for the United States in the second half of the 1970s), caused a marked divergence in the price trends of finished goods in the two countries. At 4.7 percent per year in the second half of the 1970s, the rate of increase in producer prices of Japanese manufactured goods compared favorably with the 8.7 percent annual rate of increase recorded by U.S. manufactured goods. Moreover, whereas the Japanese price trend represented a significant stabilization from the 9.0 percent annual average prevailing in the first half of the 1970s (which includes the explosive price surges of 1973–1974), the U.S. price trend worsened significantly from the 7.8 percent annual average prevailing earlier (table 4-2 and figures 4-3 and 4-4).

Table 4–2
Evolution of Producer Prices of Crude Materials and Finished Goods, and Unit Labor Costs, 1965–1981
(annual percentage changes)

	Producer Prices of Crude Materials[a]	Unit Labor Costs in Manufacturing	Producer Prices of Finished Goods
United States			
1965–1973	7.3	3.3	3.9
1973–1981	8.3	8.2	9.8
1965–1970	2.5	4.1	3.5
1970–1973	15.7	1.8	4.6
1973–1975	6.4	11.0	13.0
1975–1981	8.4	7.4	8.7
Japan			
1967–1973	3.6	6.2	3.5
1973–1981	10.9	3.9	7.2
1967–1970	1.7	3.7	2.0
1970–1973	5.5	8.8	5.0
1973–1975	19.8	20.2	14.9
1975–1981	8.1	– .1	4.7

Sources: Japan: Bank of Japan, *Economic Statistics Annual* (various issues), and table 4–1. United States: Department of Commerce, *Handbook of Cyclical Indictors* (May 1977) and *Business Conditions Digest* (various issues), and table 4–1.

[a]The Japanese index includes the prices of both crude and manufactured inputs.

Major Factors behind the Divergent Wage Behavior

The divergence in the wage behavior in the United States and Japan after the 1974–1975 disturbances can be seen even more vividly when the current year change in the wage rate is contrasted with the combined rate of change in consumer prices and labor productivity of the preceding year. The latter is the maximum rate of wage increase that can be justified from the labor point of view, and it is also the maximum rate that can be afforded from the management point of view without causing an acceleration in the prices of end products or a deterioration in corporate profit margins.[1] With the sharp rise in the inflation of material inputs that occurred in 1973–1974, the actual rate of wage increase must be restrained well below this maximum rate if the pass-through of input inflation to output prices or the deterioration in corporate profit margins is to be contained.

The average maximum rate of wage increases estimated for the United States was 10.2 percent per year for the period from 1974 to 1980. Thus, the actual increase of 9.8 percent per year came quite close to the maximum rate, in labor's favor. The resulting ratio of actual to maximum rate, 0.96,

Index

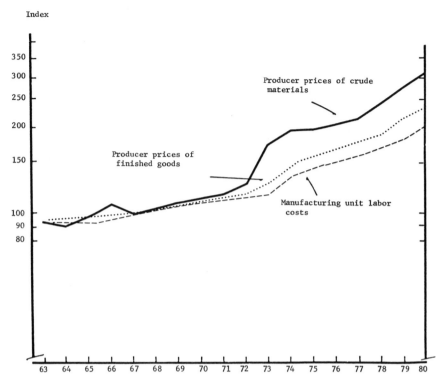

Figure 4-3. U.S. Indexes of Producer Prices of Crude Materials and Finished Goods, and of Manufacturing Unit Labor Costs, 1963–1980 (1967 = 100)

for the post-oil shock period exceeded that estimated for the preceding twelve years, 0.85. This indicated that inclusive of the excessive wage adjustment that occurred in 1974–1975, there was no moderation in wage behavior in the United States during the post-oil shock period. Although the estimated ratio for the 1976–1981 period, 0.87, declined sharply from the abnormal 1974–1975 ratio of 1.49, that ratio approximated the average of the 1960s and therefore should be considered as a return to normal conditions after the aberration of wage control in 1971–1973 and subsequent reactions (table 4-3).

By contrast, the actual annual average rate of wage increase that took place in Japan from 1974 to 1981 (11.1 percent) ran well below the estimated maximum rate (17.1 percent), resulting in a sharp reduction of the actual-to-maximum ratio (0.65) from the value estimated for the preceding twelve years (0.96). The moderation of Japanese wage behavior in the post-oil shock period was reflected particularly in the extremely low actual-to-maximum

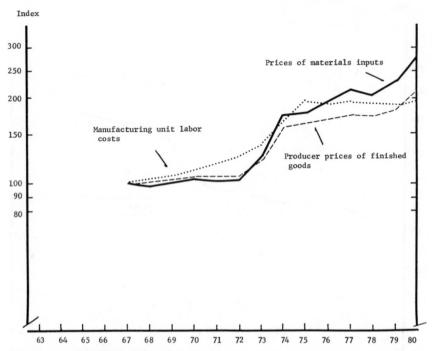

Figure 4-4. Japanese Indexes of Producer Prices of Materials Inputs and
Finished Goods, and of Manufacturing Unit Labor Costs,
1963–1980 (1967 = 100)

ratio (0.48) estimated for the 1976–1981 period. During this period,
Japanese wage adjustment barely covered cost-of-living increases, leaving
sizable productivity gains to offset the sharp rise in the prices of material inputs. The moderation of Japanese wage behavior after the 1974–1975
disturbances was a reversal from the more aggressive behavior in the late
1960s and early 1970s when the actual-to-maximum ratio had continued to
increase under a tightened labor market (table 4–3).

   Why was there a marked moderation of wage behavior in Japan after
the 1974–1975 disturbances but not in the United States? At least two major
factors may have accounted for the divergence in wage behavior. The first
was economic in nature, the second institutional.

   The acceleration in nominal wage growth in the United States occurred
in the context of a strong recovery in domestic demand after the 1974–1975
recession. Following a steep decline in 1975, the rate of capacity utilization
in manufacturing (based on the Federal Reserve series) recovered steadily
from 1976 through 1979 when it reached 85.7 percent, near the previous

Table 4–3
Comparison of Actual Rate of Increase in Hourly Compensation in Manufacturing with Combined Rate of Increase in Cost of Living and Real Output per Man-Hour in Manufacturing in the Preceding Year, 1961–1981
(annual percentage changes)

	Manufacturing Hourly Compenstion, Actual Rate (1)	Preceding Year		(2) plus (3) (4)	Ratio (1)/(4) (5)
		Cost of Living[a] (2)	Real Output per Man-Hour in Manufacturing (3)		
United States					
1961–1973	5.3	2.9	3.3	6.2	.85
1973–1981	9.8	8.8	1.4	10.2	.96
1961–1965	3.7	1.1	4.2	5.3	.70
1965–1970	6.0	3.4	2.5	5.9	1.02
1970–1973	6.2	4.5	3.5	8.0	.78
1973–1975	11.2	8.5	−1.0	7.5	1.49
1975–1981	9.4	8.9	1.9	10.8	.87
Japan					
1961–1973	15.2	5.7	10.2	15.9	.96
1973–1981	11.1	9.9	7.2	17.1	.65
1961–1965	13.6	5.9	9.7	15.6	.87
1965–1970	15.0	5.3	11.3	16.6	.90
1970–1973	18.0	6.0	8.9	14.9	1.21
1973–1975	23.9	17.9	7.1	25.0	.96
1975–1981	7.1	7.4	7.3	14.7	.48

Sources: See table 4–1.
[a]Based on consumer price index.

peak of 87.6 percent in 1973 (figure 4–5). By contrast, the slowdown of wage growth in Japan took place in conjunction with a protracted recession in the domestic economy. In the years after 1975, the recovery of capacity utilization in manufacturing was much slower and weaker in Japan than in the United States (figure 4–6).

Reflecting the difference in the strength of economic recovery, the growth of employment was maintained at a much higher rate in the United States than in Japan. Between 1973 and 1981, total civilian employment increased by 2.1 percent per annum in the United States compared to a mere 0.7 percent per annum in Japan. Although the employment situation was much bleaker in the manufacturing sector, it nevertheless remained unchanged between 1973 and 1981 in the United States despite cyclical fluctuations in between, while declining by as much as 4.0 percent in Japan (table 4–4).

U.S. wage behavior changed very little despite a large fluctuation in the civilian unemployment rate. This contrasted sharply with the Japanese

Figure 4-5. U.S. Unemployment Rate and Manufacturing Capacity Utilization, 1961–1980

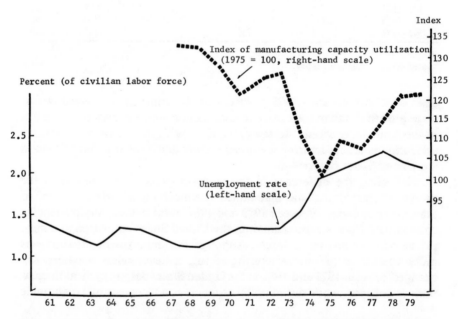

Figure 4-6. Japanese Unemployment Rate and Manufacturing Capacity Utilization, 1961–1980

Table 4–4
Total and Manufacturing Employment, 1960–1981
(annual percentage changes)

	United States		Japan	
	Total Civilian	Manufacturing	Total	Manufacturing
1960–1973	1.9	1.4	1.3	3.3
1973–1981	2.1	.0	.7	−.5
1960–1965	1.6	1.5	1.2	4.0
1965–1970	2.0	1.4	1.5	3.7
1970–1973	2.4	1.4	1.1	1.6
1973–1975	.4	−4.7	−.4	−3.4
1975–1981	2.6	1.7	1.1	.5

Sources: United States: Council of Economic Advisers, *Economic Indicators* (July 1981) and *1980 Supplement to Economic Indicators*; Japan: Ministry of Labor, *Labor Statistics Handbook* (1982).

situation, where moderation in wage behavior occurred despite the fact that the unemployment rate increased only moderately. Admittedly, the reported unemployment statistics cannot be compared directly because of certain differences in the definition of unemployment.[2] However, according to expert estimates, the adjustment of Japanese statistics to U.S. definitions did not materially change the original series.[3] They still showed that the Japanese unemployment rates were only a fraction of the U.S. rates for all the years under review. Although further adjustments (such as adding the discouraged female workers who have withdrawn from the labor market during the cyclical trough) can increase the Japanese unemployment rate,[4] it appeared that the significant disparity in the level of unemployment between the two countries resulted less from differences in the definition of unemployment than from social practices governing employment. While differences in the level of the unemployment rate are important, the analysis here focuses on changes in the rate of unemployment.[5]

The U.S. unemployment rate, after hitting a postwar peak of 8.5 percent in 1975, steadily declined in the following years, bottoming out at 5.5 percent in 1979 before climbing sharply again during the 1980 recession. In contrast, Japanese unemployment increased relatively little in 1974–1975 (from 1.1 percent in 1972–1973 to 1.8 percent in 1975) but continued to rise moderately over the years until 1978, when it peaked at 2.2 percent (figures 4–5 and 4–6).

Why was there little change in U.S. wage behavior when there was a large fluctuation in the unemployment rate? Conversely, why was there a marked moderation in wage behavior in Japan when there was only a moderate increase in the unemployment rate? Apparently there was a trade-off between wage moderation and the rate of increase in the unemployment rate. The divergence in the pattern of this trade-off seems to have stemmed

from differences in the employment system and labor-management relations in the two countries. By minimizing layoffs, Japanese business
organizations were able to obtain in exchange a significant moderation of
wage demands at a time of protracted sluggishness in the growth of the
economy. In contrast, U.S. business organizations faced more difficulties
than their Japanese counterparts in obtaining wage concessions, largely
because they have more freedom to lay off workers.

This difference in wage and employment behavior is deeply rooted in
the divergent employment systems and unionism practiced in the two countries. Under the lifetime employment system practiced by large corporations
and government agencies in Japan, employees join an organization im-
mediately after graduation from universities or high schools. Changes of
employment at midcareer are rare. Employees are hired for their long-term
potential, not for their immediate usefulness. On joining an organization,
they are given ample opportunities for on-the-job training and rotation of
posts to gain experience. Except for very serious mishaps, employees are not
fired, and their ranks and salaries increase in steps with increasing seniority
in the organization. Under this system, the employees' long-term welfare is
intimately tied to the health and growth of the organization. Therefore, just
as companies do not casually lay off employees, employees do not ask for
unreasonable compensation in times of corporate difficulties.

In comparison with the Japanese system, U.S. organizations recruit
both new graduates and experienced workers for their regular positions,
and they tend to hire employees more for their current worth than for their
long-term potential. Promotions within an organization are not orderly,
and vacancies are open to applicants from other organizations. Under such
circumstances, there is little emotional attachment between employers and
employees, who freely change jobs to seek compensation commensurate
with their own perceived worth.[6] Although a large proportion of U.S.
workers end up being employed by the same company for many years, there
is no moral obligation on either party to sustain such a relationship, and so
U.S. workers have little job security except where it is explicitly negotiated
under collective bargaining.[7]

Because of this difference in the employment system, the nature of
labor unions also differs widely between the two countries. Most Japanese
unions are enterprise unions; one becomes a member only after being employed by a particular company. In contrast, U.S. workers are often required to join the local branch of a national union before becoming eligible
for employment. Whereas the rights of Japanese workers are based mostly
on unwritten social conventions and require no protection from the labor
union, those of the U.S. workers are gained through, and protected by, collective bargaining. Therefore Japanese labor-management relations tend to
be more accommodative than confrontational, whereas the reverse is true

for the U.S. counterpart. This explains why in times of corporate difficulties, U.S. firms often cope by cutting the number of employees, while Japanese firms adjust by restraining the growth of employee compensation. It also explains why U.S. labor unions are less willing to accept a cutback in compensation without an exchange for job security.[8]

Not all Japanese employees or workers are under the protection of the lifetime employment system. Most female workers, nearly 40 percent of the labor force, are not. In fact, only regular male employees in large corporations are entitled to such protection. Including government employees who enjoy similar privileges, the total number may not exceed more than one-third of the labor force.[9] Nevertheless, it is the modern corporate sector that sets the pattern for wage movement in Japan (particularly during the tight market conditions in the 1960s), just as it is the unionized sector that sets the pattern in the United States, although the proportion of union members might not exceed one-third of the labor force.

Another factor that has contributed to the divergence in wage behavior between the two countries is the difference in the length of period covered by collective wage bargaining. Compared to the Japanese system of annual wage bargaining, a three-year cycle of contract renegotiations dominates the pattern of collective bargaining in the U.S. private business sector. Because of the coincidence of a large number of contract renegotiations in years of cyclical peak in economic activity, such as 1973 and 1979, combined with the increased use of the escalator clause for cost-of-living adjustment, wage movements in the ensuing years apparently displayed much less sensitivity to the downturn of economic activity than otherwise would have been the case.[10] This happened in both 1974–1975 and 1980–1982, except that more wage concessions resulted from the second experience, apparently because of the more protracted nature of the recent recession.

The divergence of union wage behavior in the two countries after the first oil shock can be illustrated as follows. In Japan, the moderation of union wage demands in the period since 1975 is indicated by the steep decline in the ratio of wage increase demanded (in the annual spring wage offensive) to the maximum wage increase justifiable (the preceding year's cost-of-living increase plus labor productivity growth).[11] For the period from 1977 to 1979, this ratio declined to 0.7 to 0.8, from 1.7 to 2.2 in 1972–1974 and 1.1 in 1975–1976 (figure 4–7). Moreover, the actual annual wage increase obtained declined even more sharply, running well below the rate warranted on the basis of the preceding year's cost-of-living increase and productivity growth. In the United States, from 1974 to 1980, median wage adjustments obtained from collective bargaining agreements (covering 1,000 or more workers) in the manufacturing and nonfarm business sectors amounted to 0.94 and 0.97, respectively, of the combined rates of increase in the cost of living and real output per man-hour (of the respective sector)

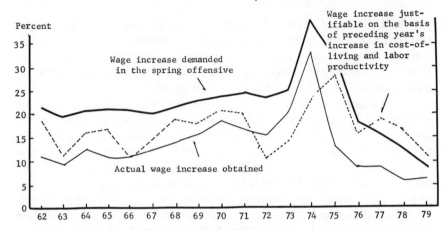

Figure 4-7. Japanese Wage Increases Demanded in Annual Spring Offensives, Wage Increases Justifiable on the Basis of Preceding Year's Increase in Cost of Living and Output per Hour, and Actual Wage Increases Obtained, 1962–1979 (annual percentage changes)

in the preceding year (table 4–5). Both ratios were higher than those estimated for the preceding twelve years, even though they were slightly lower than the ratio estimated for the manufacturing sector as a whole (0.98, shown in table 4–3). Both ratios declined in the second half of the 1970s after a sharp jump in 1974–1975, but the decline was more pronounced for the manufacturing sector than for the broader nonfarm business sector because productivity growth in the nonfarm business sector declined even more than in the manufacturing sector (table 4–5). However, as the recession dragged on and the unemployment rate continued to climb in 1981–1982 (reaching 10.8 percent by December 1982), there occurred a marked weakening in union wage demands relative to the combined measure of cost of living and productivity changes.

Differences in Wage and Price Behavior between Large Corporations and the Small Business Sector

Whereas there was a divergence in wage behavior between the modern corporate sector in Japan and the unionized sectors in the United States in response to a slowdown of economic growth after the 1974–1975 disturbances, the relative wage behavior of the small business sector or the unionized sectors in both countries was much more similar. Labor markets

Table 4–5

U.S. Effective Wage Increases Obtained by Collective Bargaining Units Compared with the Combined Rate of Increase in Cost of Living and Real Output per Man-Hour in Preceding Year, 1961–1981

(annual percentage changes)

	Effective Wage Changes Obtained for the Year		Cost of Living Plus Real Output per Man-Hour[b]		Ratio	
	Manufacturing *(1)*	*Private Nonfarm*[a] *(2)*	*Manufacturing* *(3)*	*Private Nonfarm* *(4)*	*(1)/(3)* *(5)*	*(2)/(4)* *(6)*
1961–1973	4.4	4.9	6.2	5.3	0.71	0.92
1973–1980	9.2	8.6	9.8	8.9	.94	.97
1961–1965	2.7	3.0	5.3	4.0	.51	.75
1965–1970	4.7	5.2	5.9	5.5	.80	.95
1970–1973	6.3	7.1	8.0	7.8	.79	.91
1973–1975	9.9	9.1	7.5	8.7	1.32	1.05
1975–1980	8.9	8.4	10.8	9.0	8.82	.93
1981	9.4	9.5	13.7	12.6	.69	.75

Sources: U.S. Department of Labor, *Handbook of Labor Statistics* (1981), *Monthly Labor Review* (December 1982).

Note: Median effective adjustments for the year concerned; includes both positive and negative changes.

[a]Collective bargaining units with 1,000 or more workers.

[b]The growth of productivity is based on estimates for the respective sector as a whole.

in these sectors tended to be more competitive and fluid than in the corporate or the highly unionized sectors in both countries. This led to an improvement of the relative wage position for workers in these sectors in the 1960s when the unemployment rate was lower and an excess demand condition prevailed. This situation was reversed in the second half of the 1970s when the unemployment rate was higher and an excess supply condition prevailed.

This was true in both countries,[12] but the tendency may have been much stronger in Japan than in the United States because of the greater diversity in wage and technology levels that prevailed between the modern corporate sector and the small business sector in Japan.[13] Under the tighter labor market situation of the 1960s, wage costs for smaller firms in Japan tended to rise faster than for large corporations because of lower productivity growth, resulting in a rapid reduction of wage differentials between the two sectors. This process was reversed in the second half of the 1970s because of a slackening in the labor market conditions. Thus, the ratio in wage payments of firms with thirty to ninety employees to those with five hundred or more employees increased from 58.9 percent in 1960 to 69.6 percent in 1965 and 70.8 percent in 1973. Since then, however, this ratio has declined to 66.4 percent in 1979.

This reversal in trend of the relative wage was significant from the view of price stabilization because it was the rise in the relative wage cost of the small business sector that caused a steady rise in Japan's consumer prices in the 1960s, despite stable wholesale prices for goods produced by the more efficient modern corporate sector. The decline in the small business sector's relative wage position in the second half of the 1970s, therefore, contributed to the gradual stabilization of consumer prices during this period. In fact, from 1966 to 1973, the output prices of smaller firms increased by 6.3 percent per year, compared to a mere 1.7 percent per year for the output prices of large corporations. In contrast, between 1974 and 1980, the output prices of smaller firms increased at a rate slightly lower than those of the large corporations: 6.5 percent per year versus 7.6 percent per year (figure 4-8).

Reassessment of Japanese and U.S. Employment Systems

It is clear that other than the impact of a more protracted recession, differences in the employment system and labor-management relations apparently have contributed to a marked moderation of wage and price behavior in Japan since 1975. Could this mean that the Japanese labor and employment system is preferable to the U.S. system from the macroeconomic point of view? It would be so if the moderation in wage and price behavior in Japan was attained without the cost of a protracted recession. Since this was not the case, the question remains: could the marked moderation in wage and price behavior have taken place without a protracted recession? This is an empirical question for which there is no clear-cut answer. In fact, the Japanese authorities were not sure of it, and that explains why in the wake of the second oil shock the Bank of Japan implemented a preemptive tightening of monetary policy in 1979, despite the existence of substantial excess capacities in the Japanese economy.

A related question is: can a similarly marked moderation in wage and price behavior occur in the United States if the authorities allow a protracted recession to develop, as in Japan? Some wage concessions did occur in the United States during the deep recession of 1974–1975, but the impact on wage movements was largely transitory because the recession was quickly followed by a strong recovery. More pronounced wage concessions were generated by the protracted 1980–1982 recession, but it is too early to tell whether this will result in longer-lasting changes in union wage behavior as in Japan.[14] Rather than speculate on this, we should ask the following questions: (1) what are the merits and demerits of the Japanese labor and employment system? (2) What is the problem with the U.S. system? (3) What can be done to modify U.S. wage and price behavior to make it more responsive to macroeconomic policy needs?

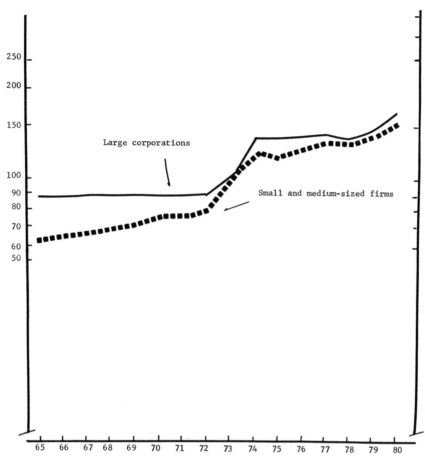

Figure 4-8. Japanese Producer Prices of Finished Goods Produced by Large and Small Firms, 1965–1980 (index, with 1973 = 100)

The merits of the Japanese system appear to include its ability to generate moderation in wage and price behavior despite a relatively low unemployment rate and its ability to keep the unemployment rate low despite a protracted recession. In comparison, the problem with the U.S. system appears to be its inability to reduce substantially the relatively high unemployment rate even under favorable economic conditions and its failure to generate a marked moderation in wage and price behavior despite the existence of a very high rate of unemployment. An additional problem with the U.S. system is that the minimum unemployment rate has ratcheted up at each peak of business cycle during the last decade, from 3.5 to 4.0 percent in the second half of the 1960s to 5.0 to 5.5 percent in 1972–1973 and around 6.0 percent in 1978–1979 (figure 4–5).

The fact that the unemployment rate was kept low despite a protracted recession and a low level of capacity utilization implied the presence of widespread underemployment or hidden unemployment in Japan during the second half of the 1970s. This was reflected in several developments, including the widely known practice of assigning temporary excess workers to do maintenance or incidental work; the sharper dip in average monthly hours for regular workers during 1974–1975 compared to a milder decline in their employment (figure 4–9); and the sharper than usual decline of the female participation rate between 1974 and 1976 (figure 2–3).[15] As sluggishness in economic activity continued, however, excess workers became a burden to corporate finance despite government subsidies for maintaining the employment status of workers temporarily laid off.[16] This led to the termination of temporary workers and the reduced recruitment of new graduates, as well as a reduction in the rate of wage and salary increase based on the length of service. Although outright dismissals of regular workers are rather rare even for smaller firms, prolonged restraint on new hiring while older workers were being retired resulted in a continued decline in regular employment for the manufacturing sector, while the average hours worked by regular workers made a slow, gradual recovery (table 4–6 and figure 4–9).

In contrast with the situation in Japan, the persistence of a high unemployment rate in the United States at cyclical peaks in economic activity apparently reflected the fact that, first, people changed jobs either voluntarily or involuntarily more often in the United States than in Japan, and, second, there has been serious structural unemployment in the United States. This is indicated by the fact that U.S. unemployment rates for such key groups as men twenty years and over and experienced wage and salary workers in a cyclical peak year, say 1973, were three to four times higher than unemployment rates for comparable groups in Japan. Moreover, unemployment rates for these groups rose during each cyclical peak and trough during the last decade (table 4–7). Several factors may have contributed to this. First, there is the widely acclaimed impact of vastly improved unemployment insurance benefits. Second, the rapid increase in the share of service employment may have raised the overall job turnover rate. Third, the dispersion of unemployment rates between regions may have increased because of an observed decline in the trend of people and families moving around the country, which appears to have occurred in conjunction with the rapid increase in the female participation rate and in the number of two-worker families. Meanwhile job opportunities may have changed at widely differing rates between regions because of increased foreign competition and the large change in relative price caused by repeated oil shocks.

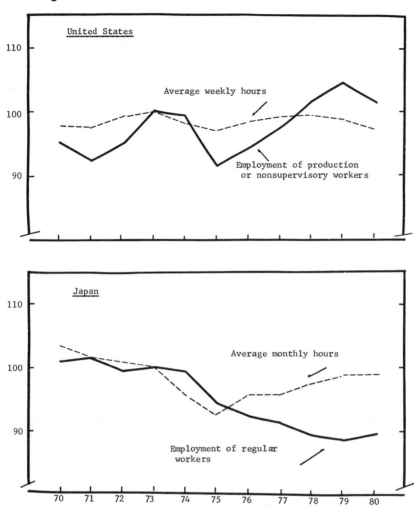

Figure 4-9. Employment of Regular Workers and Average Weekly or
Monthly Hours in Manufacturing, 1970–1980 (index, with
1973 = 100)

These developments must have contributed to the widely observed phenomenon of certain industries and regions experiencing shortages of skilled
labor while other industries or regions were suffering from severe depres-
sions and high unemployment.

Nevertheless, abstracting from the problem of structural unemployment,
there was a trade-off between explicit unemployment and hidden underemployment. Thus, in contrast with the situation in Japan, manufacturing

Table 4-6
Relative Popularity of Various Methods Used in Reducing Worker
Redundancy in the Machinery Industry, Japan, 1974–1976
(percentage of firms surveyed)

	Larger Firms[a]			Smaller Firms[a]		
	1974	1975	1976	1974	1975	1976
Restricting overtime	61.3	90.3	80.6	39.2	74.3	55.4
Reducing new recruitment	35.5	77.4	80.6	21.6	52.7	67.6
Stop filling vacancies	35.6	67.7	71.0	23.0	60.8	55.4
Transferring to other posts within plant	48.4	64.5	64.5	35.1	64.9	52.7
Transferring to other plants	51.6	77.4	74.2	23.0	45.9	50.0
Transferring to subsidiaries	48.4	61.3	58.1	16.2	23.0	14.9
Dismissal of temporary workers	2.9	41.9	29.0	21.6	48.6	14.9
Temporary layoff of regular workers	38.7	38.7	6.5	10.8	36.5	6.8
Soliciting early retirement	6.5	.0	.0	8.1	14.9	6.8
Selective dismissals	.0	.0	.0	2.7	1.4	1.4

Source: Haruo Shimada, "The Japanese Labor Market after the Oil Crisis: A Factual Report," *Keio Economic Studies* 14 (1977):62. The original data are based on unpublished interim results of a survey on intrafirm labor mobility organized by the Ministry of International Trade and Industry and managed by Professor S. Matsushima.

[a]Larger firms are those listed in the First Section of Tokyo Stock Exchange; smaller firms are those listed in the Second Section of the same exchange. The sample includes thirty-one larger firms and seventy-four smaller firms.

employment dropped sharply in the United States during the 1975 recession while average weekly hours declined only moderately (figure 4-9). This leads to the question, Which is more desirable in a cyclical downturn: to have more explicit unemployment as in the United States or to have less explicit unemployment but more hidden underemployment as in Japan?

Table 4-7
Unemployment Rate, by Selected Groups and for Selected Years
(percent of civilian labor force in group)

	United States					Japan		
	1969	1973	1975	1979	1982	1973	1975	1978
Total	3.5	4.9	8.5	5.8	9.7	1.3	1.9	2.2
Men 20 years and over	2.1	3.3	6.8	4.2	8.8	1.2	1.9	2.3
Both sexes, 16–19 years	12.2	14.5	19.9	16.1	23.2	2.8	3.0	4.6
Blacks and other minorities	6.4	8.9	13.9	11.3	17.3			
Share of service employment[a]	48.1	49.7	51.5	52.8	56.1	46.4	48.2	50.1

Sources: United States: Department of Commerce, *1980 Supplement to Economic Indicators* (Washington, D.C., 1980). Japan: Ministry of Labor, *Labor Statistics Yearbook* (various issues) (Tokyo).

[a]Includes transportation and public utilities, wholesale and retail trade, finance, real estate, and other services but excludes all levels of government.

From the microeconomic point of view, the U.S. system, with the freedom to lay off employees when the need arises, appears to be more conducive to the efficient allocation of labor. However, this is not necessarily so because lack of job security tends to make labor unions less flexible on wage cutbacks and other issues of importance to corporate management (such as the option of increasing subcontracting to reduce production cost). In consequence, management may continue to face wage pressures despite a cutback in the number of employees and may also fall short of making all the adjustments in operations necessary for corporate rejuvenation.[17] The result is higher unemployment but without the benefit of wage moderation. Thus the U.S. system appears less efficient from the macroeconomic point of view although it may appear more efficient from the microeconomic point of view.

In contrast, under the lifetime employment system practiced by the modern corporate sector in Japan, there is a congruence of interests between employees and management. Because of this, corporate management has more freedom to introduce measures to cut production costs and to improve labor productivity, although it cannot lay off employees at will. The result is a moderation in wage behavior in times of corporate difficulties but without much of an increase in the unemployment rate. Although the wage bill is relatively inflexible except for bonus payments, this is offset over time by the improvement in labor productivity, as exemplified by the experience in the late 1970s. It appears that the Japanese employment system, while being relatively rigid and hence inefficient from the microeconomic point of view, is quite flexible and efficient from the macroeconomic point of view.

Nevertheless, the Japanese system is not without problems, particularly when sluggish economic growth becomes a permanent feature. In such a case, a lack of flexibility for adjusting the number of employees becomes a burden to corporate management, and the morale of employees can be affected by the diminishing opportunities for promotion. An increase in labor mobility between sectors may then become necessary. Mindful of these problems, Japanese industries have been trying to control the numbers of regular male employees while using more temporary workers to meet the fluctuation in business demand (figure 4-10).[18] Largely automatic increases in wages and salaries based on length of service have been reduced under the pressures of a protracted slowdown in the economy as well as an increase in the average age of employees. Although mandatory retirement at age fifty-five is being extended because of increased life expectancies, this has been done with reduced pay and changes in posts in order to minimize the burden on the wage bill and also to avoid disturbing the system of orderly promotions. However, the essence of the Japanese system lies in its commitment to lifetime employment. This feature of the system continues to receive wide support from both management and employees despite the protracted recession in the second half of the 1970s.[19]

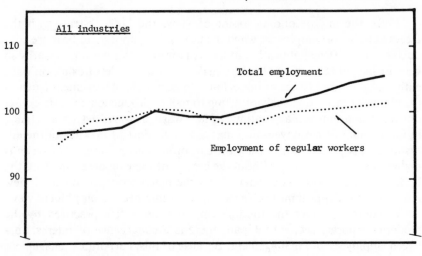

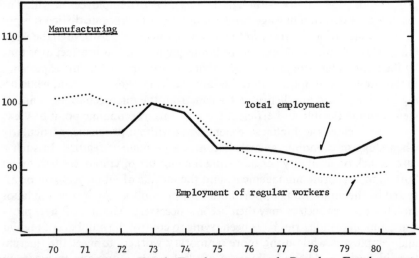

Figure 4-10. Japanese Total Employment and Regular Employment, 1970–1980 (index, with 1973 = 100)

As the U.S. economy suffered another deep recession in 1980–1981 without a marked deceleration in price inflation, the question inevitably arises, Will it be possible to modify U.S. wage-price behavior in the light of the Japanese experience? Since both the U.S. and Japanese employment systems are products of long-term evolution peculiar to the respective society, it is neither possible nor desirable to copy another system in its entirety; however, it may be possible to make U.S. labor-management relations less confrontational and more collaborative if management can offer job security in exchange for wage moderation. This can be promoted by government policy. In order to minimize excessive unemployment in cyclical downturns, large businesses in distress can be encouraged to retain employees through the reduction of payroll taxes and granting of tax credits for wage payments for employees who would be laid off otherwise. The duration of the tax reduction and tax credits can be limited to the period for which the firms can produce evidence of business distress, and the amount of the tax reduction and tax credits can be limited to the amount of unemployment insurance payments entitled by the employees who otherwise would be laid off. Under such an arrangement, firms may operate more flexible work hours for a more stable work force, the economy will be less burdened by the unemployed, and society may remain more cohesive.

Notes

1. This is based on the expectation that trends in productivity growth, nonwage production costs, and sales volume will remain the same.

2. For example, the inclusion of temporary layoffs in U.S. statistics and their exclusion in Japan. Also in contrast with the U.S. practice, where there is no sharp distinction between a temporary layoff and a permanent termination of employment, Japanese workers temporarily laid off are not considered terminated from their employment and do not look for work elsewhere.

3. Joyanna Moy and Constance Sorrentino, "Unemployment, Labor Force Trends, and Layoff Practices in 10 Countries," *Monthly Labor Review* (December 1981):5.

4. See, for example, Akira Ono, "Keiki Kotai to Rodo Shijo" (Recession and the labor market), in Kenjiro Ara, ed., *Sengo Keizai Seisaku Ron no Soten* (Controversies on postwar economic policies) (Tokyo: Keiso Shobo, 1980), pp. 322–327.

5. For the reasons why the U.S. unemployment rate was much higher than in Japan and the European countries, see Roger Kauman, "Why the U.S. Unemployment Is So High," in Michael J. Piore, ed., *Unemployment and Inflation: Institutionalist and Structuralist Views* (Armonk, New York: M.E. Sharpe, 1979), pp. 155–169.

6. It has often been commented on that Japanese workers, when asked about what did they do, state their company affiliations (such as Mitsui or Mitsubishi) while U.S. workers state their job (such as machinist or computer analyst). See Chie Nakane, *Japanese Society* (Berkeley: University of California Press, 1970), p. 3.

7. According to a U.S. population survey, over 35 percent of U.S. workers aged fifty to fifty-four have not changed jobs for at least fifteen

years. See Robert E. Hall, "Employment Fluctuations and Wage Rigidity," *Brookings Papers on Economic Activity* (1:1980), p. 98.

8. This tendency is aggravated by the U.S. practice of laying off new workers first, which tends to make senior workers less inclined to accept wage concessions unless their own job security is threatened. In contrast, under the Japanese lifetime employment system, the job security of new recruits is ensured, and it is the older workers who are encouraged to take early retirement in times of severe corporate difficulties.

9. Kazuo Sato, in his communication with me, pointed out that the male employees in large corporations may number about one-quarter of the total labor force. For estimates in the range of 30 to 40 percent, see Ezra F. Vogel, *The Japanese Middle Class* (Berkeley: University of California Press, 1963), p. 6, and Kauman, "Why the U.S. Unemployment Rate Is so High," p. 167.

10. See Daniel J.B. Mitchell, "Recent Union Contract Concessions," *Brookings Papers on Economic Activity* (1:1982), p. 179.

11. For this estimate, productivity growth is approximated by the growth rate of real output per man-hour in manufacturing shown in table 4-1.

12. On the situation in the United States, see George L. Perry, "Slowing the Wage Price Spiral: The Macroeconomic View," *Brookings Papers on Economic Activity* (2:1978), pp. 266-267.

13. Such differentials resulted, in turn, from the rapid industrialization and the inevitable lag in the introduction of modern practices in the small business sector.

14. For details of union wage concessions, see Mitchell, "Recent Union Contract Concessions."

15. Although the female participation rate had been declining through the 1960s because of the reduction of women workers in rural households in conjunction with the rapid decline of agricultural employment, its sharper decline in 1974-1976 was widely attributed to discouragement encountered in obtaining suitable employment. See Haruo Shimada, "The Japanese Labor Market after the Oil Crisis: A Factual Report," in *Keio Economic Studies* 14 (1977):40-42; and Ono, "Keki Kotai." Since 1976, however, there has been an increase in the female participation rate in the twenty-five to thirty-nine age group. See Economic Planning Agency, *Keizai Hakusho, 1981* (White paper on the economy) (Tokyo: Economic Planning Agency, 1981), pp. 154-155.

16. Workers temporarily laid off received about 90 percent of their normal pay. In turn, the employers were subsidized by the government for one-half (in the case of large firms) or two-thirds (in the case of small firms) of their wage payments to the laid-off workers. See Shimada, "Japanese Labor Market," pp. 46-47.

17. In fact, some of the major declining industries in the United States (such as automobiles and steel) continued to suffer from an upward bias in wage rates in relation to industrial average while failing to make the necessary investments to improve their productivity.

18. For a detailed discussion of employment adjustment problems in Japan after the oil shock, see Thomas P. Rohlen, " 'Permanent Employment' Faces Recession, Slow Growth, and an Aging Work Force," *Journal of Japanese Studies* 5 (Summer 1979).

19. Seventy to 80 percent of those polled expressed support for lifetime employment and enterprise unionism. They also expected the system to continue in the 1980s. However, over 40 percent did not express support for the automatic increase in wage and rank and over 80 percent expected the system to change in the future. See Economic Planing Agency, *Keizai Hakusho* (The white paper on the economy) (Tokyo: Economic Planning Agency, 1980), pp. 305–330.

5 Major Factors
Underlying Contrasting
Productivity Trends
before and after the
Oil Shock

In addition to the helpful moderation of wage behavior, the competitiveness of unit labor costs in Japanese industry has also been aided by rapid growth in labor productivity. This was true not only in the postwar decades before the first oil shock but also afterward during a period of lower economic growth. In terms of growth in labor productivity, Japan consistently outperformed the other industrial countries during the first two postwar decades. Most curiously, however, productivity growth during the late 1960s accelerated in Japan while decelerating in the United States. In the aftermath of the first oil shock, U.S. productivity growth has resumed its decline following a brief recovery while Japan's has since recovered to a relatively high rate. This chapter examines the major factors underlying these developments.

Divergence in Productivity Trends

Throughout the three decades after World War II, labor productivity rose much faster in Japan than in the United States. This was true for both the period before the first oil shock and the period after. For the decade and a half prior to 1970, real output per employee in Japan increased by 7.7 percent per year at as much as four and one-half times the rate of that in the United States (1.7 percent per year) from 1950 to 1970. Moreover, while the growth of labor productivity accelerated in Japan during the second half of the 1960s, it slowed down in the United States, resulting in a widening of growth differential. And even though the growth of Japan's labor productivity suffered a sharp decline during the 1970s (to 3.9 percent per year), the decline was even sharper in the United States (to 0.8 percent per year). In particular, in the seven years since 1974, the growth of real output per employee declined to a mere 0.2 percent per year in the United States while it was maintained at 3.0 percent per year in Japan—fifteen times the U.S. rate (table 5–1).

This divergence in productivity growth between the United States and Japan is observed regardless of whether the government sector is included or excluded.[1] In the private economy, greater differentials in productivity growth are found for the nonfarm sectors than for the agricultural sector. In the manufacturing sector especially, the differential has widened since the first oil shock.

Table 5-1
Growth in Real Output per Employee by Sectors and Periods: Japanese Growth Rate in Relation to U.S. Growth Rate

	Total	Private Sector	Manufacturing	Agriculture, Forestry, and Fishery	Other Private
1960–1970	4.1	3.6	3.5	1.0	3.8
1970–1980	4.9	3.7	2.8	1.6	4.0
1965–1970	5.4	5.1	5.4	1.4	
1970–1973	4.5	3.4	2.0	4.7	4.3
1973–1980	15.0	15.0	16.5	.4	
1975–1980	5.4	4.4	5.1	.4	2.2

Sources: Tables 5–2 and 5–3.

Note: Shown as a ratio of Japanese growth rate to U.S. growth rate. Empty cells indicate that the ratio cannot be computed because of a negative U.S. growth rate.

Another feature of this comparison in productivity concerns the relative rate of growth between output and employment. In both countries the growth of real output showed a downward trend in the 1970s after an upward trend in the 1960s. However, the growth of employment began diverging in the 1960s, accelerating in the United States but decelerating in Japan. During the 1970s, Japanese employment increased by less than 1 percent per year, while U.S. employment increased by nearly 2.5 percent per year. In both countries employment increased rapidly in the service sectors and in the government sector throughout the postwar decades; however, trends in manufacturing employment differed widely between the two countries, increasing much faster in Japan during the 1950s and 1960s but slowing down much more sharply in Japan than in the United States during the 1970s. During the latest decade, manufacturing employment declined somewhat in Japan and increased by 0.5 percent per year in the United States. Also, in both countries the agricultural labor force shrank by as much as 3 to 4 percent per year during the 1950s and 1960s, but this decline slowed in the United States during the 1970s while continuing at a reduced but relatively high rate in Japan (tables 5–2 and 5–3).

In summary, the large differential in productivity growth between the two countries during the 1950s and the 1960s was caused primarily by a higher rate of output growth in Japan despite a similar pace of employment growth. However, the widening of this differential during the 1970s was caused by a slowdown of output growth despite an acceleration of employment growth in the United States. In comparison, the rate of output growth declined even more in Japan during the 1970s, but the tempo of productivity growth was maintained at a relatively high rate because of a proportionate decline in the rate of employment growth. These tendencies were true for the economy as a whole and were related to developments in the private nonfarm sector, particularly in manufacturing.

Table 5-2
Growth of U.S. Real Output, Employment, and Real Output per
Employee, by Selected Sectors and Periods, 1950-1980
(annual percentage changes)

	Total	Private Sector	Manufac- turing	Agri- culture	Other Private	Govern- ment
GNP (in 1972 prices)						
1950-1970	3.6	4.3	3.5	0.8	3.8	3.8
1960-1970	3.9	4.0	4.3	.7	4.1	3.6
1970-1980	3.2	3.4	3.0	1.6	3.6	1.3
1965-1969	4.0	3.9	4.1	.1	4.2	4.5
1969-1973	3.6	4.1	4.1	1.9	3.9	.8
1973-1980	2.4	2.5	1.1	1.9	3.1	1.6
1973-1975	− .8	− 1.2	− 5.4	2.5	.1	2.1
1975-1980	3.7	4.0	3.9	1.6	4.3	1.4
Employment						
1950-1970	1.5	1.2	1.2	− 3.6	2.1	3.6
1960-1970	1.8	1.4	1.4	− 4.4	2.1	4.2
1970-1980	2.4	2.3	.5	− .3	3.2	2.6
1965-1969	2.3	1.9	1.8	− 4.6	4.2	4.9
1969-1973	2.2	2.1	− .2	− 1.0	3.1	3.0
1973-1980	2.2	2.2	.7	− .4 .	3.2	2.4
1973-1975	.5	− .1	− 4.7	− .9	2.1	3.4
1975-1980	3.0	3.1	2.1	− .3	3.7	2.0
Real output per employee						
1950-1970	1.7	3.1	2.2	4.6	1.7	.2
1960-1970	2.1	2.6	2.9	5.3	2.0	− .6
1970-1980	.8	1.1	2.5	1.9	.4	− .3
1965-1969	1.7	2.0	2.3	4.7	.0	− .4
1969-1973	1.4	2.0	4.3	2.9	.8	− 2.1
1973-1980	.2	.2	.4	2.3	− .1	− .8
1973-1975	− 1.3	− 1.1	− .7	3.4	− 2.0	− 1.3
1975-1980	.7	.9	1.8	1.9	.6	− .6

Sources: Council of Economic Advisers, *Economic Report of the President* (February 1982);
1980 Supplement to Economic Indicators, and *Economic Indicators* (July 1981).

Growth of Capital Stock per Employee and
Changes in Capital-Output Ratio

Why, during the two decades prior to the oil shock, was Japan able to attain
a much higher rate of output growth despite a rate of employment growth
similar to that in the United States? Why, during the 1970s, did the growth
of real output fall in the United States in spite of an increase in the rate of
growth of employment? Yet during the same period Japan was able to
maintain a relatively high rate of output growth, particularly in the
manufacturing sector, with a sharp slowdown in the rate of growth of
employment. Why? This section attempts to answer these questions through
an analysis of the mechanics of productivity growth.

Table 5-3
Japanese Growth of Real Output, Employment, and Real Output per Employee, by Selected Sectors and Periods, 1955-1980
(annual percentage changes)

	Total	Private Sector	Manufac- turing	Agriculture, Forestry, and Fishery	Other Private	Govern- ment
GNP (in 1975 prices)						
1955-1970	9.9					
1960-1970	10.6	11.3	14.3	1.5	11.5	5.1
1970-1980	4.8	4.9	7.0	.3	4.0	4.0
1965-1970	11.2	12.0	16.7	1.7	11.4	4.3
1970-1973	7.4	7.8	10.3	5.2	6.7	3.5
1973-1980	3.7	3.7	5.7	-1.8	2.9	4.2
1973-1975	.6	.2	-2.9	-1.4	2.2	5.3
1975-1980	5.0	5.2	9.4	-2.0	3.7	3.8
Employment						
1955-1970	1.9	1.9	4.1	-3.3	4.0	1.7
1960-1970	1.8	1.7	3.8	-3.4	3.7	2.8
1970-1980	.9	.8	-.1	-4.2	2.4	2.1
1965-1970	1.8	1.7	3.7	-4.5	2.9	.5
1970-1973	1.0	1.0	1.6	-7.3	3.2	3.8
1973-1980	.7	.7	-.8	-2.8	2.1	1.4
1973-1975	-.3	-.5	-3.4	-3.2	1.5	.5
1975-1980	1.2	1.2	.3	-2.7	2.4	.3
Real output per employee						
1955-1970	7.9					
1960-1970	8.6	9.4	10.1	5.1	7.5	2.2
1970-1980	3.9	4.1	7.1	4.7	1.6	1.9
1965-1970	9.2	10.1	12.5	6.5	8.3	3.8
1970-1973	6.3	6.8	8.5	13.5	3.4	-.3
1973-1980	3.0	3.0	6.6	1.0	.8	2.8
1973-1975	.9	.7	.5	1.9	.7	4.8
1975-1980	3.8	4.0	9.1	0.8	1.3	3.5

Sources: Economic Planning Agency, *Keizai Yoran* (Economic data handbook) (1982). Ministry of Labor, *Rodo Tokei Yoran* (Labor statistics handbook) (1982). Organisation for Economic Cooperation and Development, *National Accounts of OECD Countries, 1950-1979* (January 1981).

Because the growth of labor productivity was spearheaded by the private nonfarm sector, particularly in manufacturing, the production of output or value added by the employee depends very much on the increase of capital stock per employee and its manner of utilization. This relationship is shown as

$$\frac{Y}{L} = \frac{K}{L} \times \frac{Y}{K}$$

where Y/L, K/L, and Y/K stand, respectively, for real output per employee, real capital stock per employee, and output-capital ratio in real terms. Apparently the higher the capital-labor ratio and the output-capital ratio are, the higher the output-labor ratio. This relationship remains true if all variables are shown as a rate of change per unit of time. Real capital stock per employee will increase rapidly only if there are strong inducements for investment. In addition, the growth of real output per unit of capital stock will remain high only if there is rapid demand growth or if the desired capital stock matches the composition of demand. In the short run, the output-capital ratio may fluctuate because of cyclical changes in demand or changes in capital efficiency, caused by structural changes in demand, supply, or technological advancements. Also, both the increase in capital stock per employee and the improvement in capital efficiency presume a concomitant improvement in the quality of labor. Without such improvement, the growth of output per unit of capital, and hence of labor, will be retarded.

Based on estimates shown in tables 5-4 and 5-5 as well as figures 5-1 and 5-2, the evolution of real capital stock per employee and capital output ratio appears as follows:

Growth of Gross Nonresidential Capital Stock per Employee: As in the growth of real output, real gross nonresidential capital stock in the private sector increased two to three times faster in Japan than in the United States during the 1950s and the 1960s. In Japan, growth in capital stock accelerated in the 1960s but decelerated during the 1970s, particularly after the first oil shock. In comparison, there was no deceleration in the United States. Given a similar rate of growth of employment in the private sector during the two decades ended 1970, per employee capital stock increased two to three times faster in Japan than in the United States. Also, because of the divergence of employment trends during the 1970s, the differential in the growth of per-employee capital stock widened to four times in Japan's favor despite a marked slowdown in the growth of capital stock in that country.

One outstanding feature of the Japanese investment pattern has been the relative concentration of capital investment in the corporate business sector, particularly in manufacturing. During the 1950s and the 1960s, the growth of capital investment in Japan was much faster in the manufacturing sector than for the private business sector as a whole, while the reverse was true for the United States. Hence, the differential in the growth of per-employee capital stock was greater for manufacturing than for the whole private business sector. For the two decades ending in 1970, the Japanese growth rate averaged more than three times faster than that of the United States; during the 1960s it was five times faster. Although this differential was reduced somewhat in the changed investment climate of the early 1970s,

Table 5-4
Growth of Real Gross Nonresidential Capital Stock per Employee in the Private Sector and in Manufacturing, 1950-1979
(annual percentage changes)

	United States		Japan	
	Total	*Manufacturing*	*Total*	*Manufacturing*
Real gross capital stock				
1950-1970	3.7	3.2	10.3[a]	13.1[a]
1960-1970 (1960-1969)	4.0 (3.5)	3.2	11.9	14.8
1970-1979 (1969-1979)	3.9 (4.4)	3.4	8.5	7.6
1975-1979	3.7	3.9	6.4	4.8
Civilian employment[b]				
1950-1970	1.2	1.2	1.9[a]	4.1[a]
1960-1970 (1960-1969)	1.5 (1.5)	1.4	1.7	3.8
1970-1979 (1969-1979)	2.5 (2.4)	.9	.7	-.4
1975-1979	3.9	3.5	1.2	-.2
Gross capital stock per employee				
1950-1970	2.4	2.0	8.2[a]	8.6[a]
1960-1970 (1960-1969)	2.5 (2.0)	1.8	10.0	10.6
1970-1979 (1969-1979)	1.4 (1.9)	2.5	7.7	8.0
1975-1979	-.1	.4	5.1	5.0
Reference items: Value in 1975				
Gross capital stock				
(billion US$ or equivalent[c])	2,471	577	673	301
Gross capital stock per				
employee (US$ equivalent)	34,725	31,480	13,388	22,363

Sources: United States: Estimated from Department of Commerce, *Survey of Current Business* (February 1981) and *1980 Supplement to Economic Indicators* Japan: Estimated from Economic Planning Agency, *National Economic Accounts Quarterly* (1980, No. 41), and *Keizai Yoran* (Economic data handbook) (1981).
[a]For 1955-1970.
[b]Excluding government employees at all levels of government.
[c]The Japanese capital stock has been converted into U.S. dollars at the rate of 305 yen per dollar.

it widened again after the first oil shock because of the divergence of employment trends in the two countries. For the period 1975 through 1979, U.S. capital stock per employee in manufacturing increased by only 0.4 percent per year compared to 5.0 percent per year for Japan, resulting in a ratio of twelve to one in Japan's favor (table 5-4).

Because of the difference in investment pattern, the manufacturing sector accounts for a much larger share of capital stock in Japan than in the United States (44 percent versus 23 percent in 1975), and although Japanese business capital stock amounted to only a little more than one-quarter of the U.S. counterpart in the United States, its manufacturing capital stock

Table 5-5
**Evolution of Real Output per Employee, Gross Capital Stock per
Employee, and Real Output per Unit of Capital in the Private Sector and
Manufacturing, 1950–1980**
(annual percentage changes)

	Private Sector[a]			Manufacturing[a]		
	Y/L	K/L	Y/K	Y/L	K/L	Y/K
United States						
1950–1970	3.1	2.4	0.6	2.2	2.0	0.3
1960–1970	2.6	2.5	.0	2.9	1.8	1.1
1970–1980[b]	1.1	1.4	−.3	2.5	2.5	.0
1965–1969	2.0	2.9	−.9	2.3	2.7	−.4
1969–1973	2.0	2.1	−.1	4.3	2.8	1.5
1973–1980[b]	.2	1.4	−1.2	.4	3.1	−2.6
1973–1975	−1.1	3.8	−4.7	−.7	8.8	−8.7
1975–1980[b]	.9	.6	.3	1.8	1.8	.0
Japan						
1955–1970		8.8			8.6	
1960–1970	9.9	10.5	−.5	10.1	10.6	−.5
1970–1980[b]	4.1	7.7	−3.3	7.1	8.0	−.8
1965–1970	10.1	10.3	−.2	12.5	10.0	2.3
1970–1973	6.8	10.7	−3.5	8.5	9.8	−1.2
1973–1980[b]	3.0	6.2	−3.0	6.6	6.5	.1
1973–1975	.7	8.4	−7.1	.5	10.8	−9.3
1975–1980[b]	4.0	5.0	−1.0	9.1	4.5	4.4

Sources: Tables 5–1 through 5–4.
[a] Y/L, K/L, and Y/K stand, respectively, for real output per employee, gross capital stock per employee, and real output per unit of capital stock.
[b] The data cover only up to 1979 for K/L. Estimates for Y/K are derived fom the relationship $Y/K = Y/L \div K/L$.

was over one-half of the U.S. stock.[2] Moreover, in terms of per-employee capital stock, the gap between the two countries has narrowed substantially over the years. In 1975, the Japanese capital stock per employee amounted to nearly 40 percent of the U.S. counterpart for all nonresidential capital and over 70 percent of the U.S. stock for the manufacturing sector (table 5–4). Given the large differential in the growth of per-employee capital stock, the gap between the two countries must have narrowed even more since then. At the relative rate of the late 1970s (5.0 percent per year versus 0.4 percent per year), the Japanese capital stock per employee in manufacturing should exceed the U.S. level by 1984.

Changes in Capital-Output Ratio: There were both similarities and dissimilarities in the movements of capital-output ratio in the two countries over the past thirty years. First, the capital-output ratio for the private sector as a whole was significantly lower for Japan than for the United States

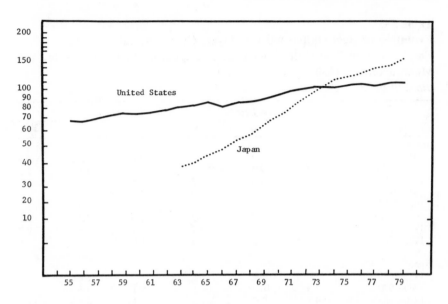

Figure 5-1. Evolution of Real, Gross Nonresidential Capital Stock per
Employee in the Private Sector, 1955–1979 (index, with 1973 =
100)

(1.2 versus 1.4 to 1.5) during the 1950s and the 1960s, but the Japanese ratio
steadily rose during the 1970s to the U.S. level. The average ratio for the
United States in the 1970s, while being significantly higher than in the 1960s
(1.5 to 1.6 versus 1.35 to 1.50), was not much higher than in the late 1950s.
In both countries there was a decline in the capital-output ratio during the
period of higher output growth in the 1960s and a rise in the ratio during the
period of lower ouput growth in the 1970s. Second, the Japanese capital-
output ratio for manufacturing was much higher than that for the private
sector as a whole during the 1960s (1.65 to 1.75 versus 1.15 to 1.25), but the
difference narrowed during the 1970s. In comparison, the U.S. capital-
output ratio for manufacturing was somewhat lower than for the private
sector as a whole during most of the 1960s and the 1970s. In both countries
the capital-output ratio for manufacturing shot up sharply during
1974–1975 before coming down, but the fluctuation was much sharper for
Japan than for the United States (figure 5–3).

The evolution of capital-output ratio (shown in the reverse form of
Y/K, real output per unit of gross capital stock) is listed in table 5–5 along
with changes in real output per employee (Y/L) and gross capital stock per
employee (K/L) for the periods under review. During the 1950s and the
1960s, the growth of real output per employee occurred largely in parallel

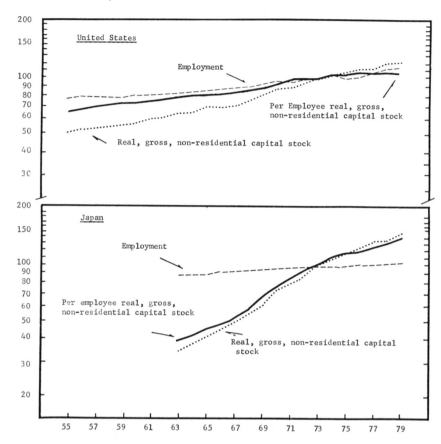

Figure 5-2. Evolution of Real, Gross Nonresidential Capital Stock, Employment, and per Employee Real Gross Nonresidential Capital Stock in the Private Sector, 1955–1979 (index, with 1973 = 100)

with the growth of capital stock per employee. This was largely true for both the United States and Japan. Thus, the difference in the rate of growth of capital stock per employee determined the gap in the rate of growth of labor productivity. Toward the end of the 1960s, however, capital productivity deteriorated in the United States but improved in Japan. This divergence in trends apparently contributed to the divergence of labor productivity between the two countries over and above the difference in the rate of growth of capital stock per employee (table 5-5).

On the contrary, during the early 1970s the trends of capital productivity moved in favor of the United States and against Japan. This caused a

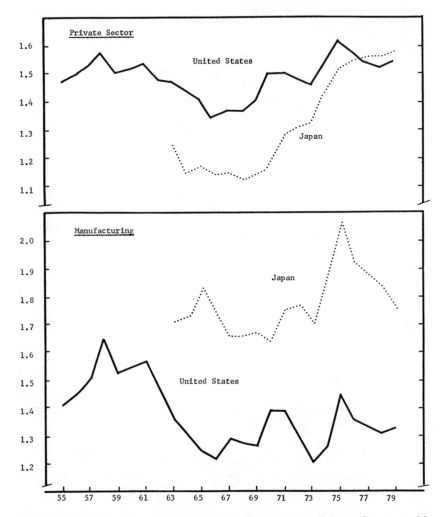

Figure 5-3. Evolution of Capital-Output Ratio in the Private Sector and in Manufacturing, 1955–1979

slowdown in the growth of Japanese labor productivity, despite the sustained growth of capital stock per employee, while facilitating an improvement in U.S. labor productivity in manufacturing. The situation changed again with the onset of the first oil shock. Both countries suffered a severe deterioration in capital productivity during 1974–1975, and labor productivity flattened out despite the continued growth of capital stock per employee. In the ensuing period, the growth of capital stock per employee declined sharply in both the United States and Japan. This constrained the recovery of the growth of labor productivity, except in the Japanese manufacturing sector where a resurgence in the growth of labor productivity was facilitated by a sharp improvement in capital productivity (table 5-5).

Causes of Divergent Investment and Productivity Behavior

Why did investment in productive capacities grow much faster in Japan than in the United States during the first two decades of the postwar era, and why in the aftermath of the first oil shock did the growth of such investment fall more abruptly in Japan than in the United States? Why did capital productivity experience different outcomes in the two countries starting from the late 1960s through the 1970s? This section attempts to explain the major economic factors underlying these changes.

Situation before the Oil Shocks

The faster growth of investment activity in Japan during the 1950s and the 1960s apparently had to do with the catching-up process of technology absorption and capital accumulation on the part of the Japanese economy. Because of wartime destruction in productive facilities suffered in Japan proper, the loss of such facilities built in former colonies, and the retardation in the development of durable consumer goods, at the end of World War II there was a large store of advanced technologies and manufactured goods for Japanese industry to absorb and to produce. Although there was also strong pent-up demand for durable consumer goods, automobiles, and housing in the United States at the end of World War II, the strength of investment demand there was perhaps not as intense as in Japan, considering that the United States was the world's technological leader and had been untouched by wartime destruction.

Postwar investment growth in Japan was facilitated by several factors. The external environment in the 1950s and the 1960s was highly conducive to a pattern of economic growth based on outward-looking development. The Bretton Woods system of stable exchange rates and increasingly freer world markets for goods, services, and financial capital gave Japan easy access to an abundant supply of imported fuels and raw materials, advanced technologies, and rapidly expanding world markets. From the mid-1950s through 1971, the real cost of oil declined and, except for brief and relatively minor fluctuations, the terms of trade were favorable to countries exporting manufactures in exchange for raw materials. In addition to the generally favorable external environment, Japan also benefited from economic booms associated with two major wars (in Korea and Vietnam) without suffering the strains of war efforts. Also the Japanese government played an active role in the promotion of investment activity and in channeling excess household savings into productive investments. Periodic assessments of the nation's development needs through preparation and publication of medium- or long-term plans were done not only for the economy as a whole but also for key sectors. None of these plans was compulsory in nature; direct government investments were limited to the construction of overhead capital facilities and railways. However, these plans served as a means of building a social consensus and for educating the general public because their preparation involved the participation of experts drawn from the ministries and industries concerned, academia, and even the mass media.

Government guidance through such key agencies as the Ministry of International Trade and Industry (MITI), the Ministry of Finance, and the Bank of Japan was also important. MITI formulated the nation's industrial policy through the advice of such organs as the Industrial Structure Council and used administrative guidance to influence the direction of plant and equipment investment. MITI's main concern has been to strengthen Japan's industrial structure and competitive position in exports. The Ministry of Finance, with the help of the Tax Advisory Commission, used special tax measures to promote saving and investment, and the Bank of Japan relied on a low interest rate policy and window guidance to control the direction and tempo of bank credit expansion. These three government agencies thus complemented each other, exercising a powerful influence on the direction of Japan's postwar industrialization.

Throughout the 1950s and the 1960s, Japan was able to take full advantage of the favorable world economic environment to attain extremely high rates of growth of investment, exports, and economic growth. By maintaining a high savings ratio, at least twice that of the United States, and by devoting most of this to reequip its well-educated labor force with increasingly sophisticated productive equipment, Japan was able to close rapidly the gap in per-capita stock of productive capital. In the fifteen years from 1955 to 1970, Japan's gross nonresidential capital stock per employee increased by 8.8 percent per year in real terms, more than three and a half times the U.S. rate. The differential in growth rate widened even more in the 1960s, particularly in the manufacturing sector. During that decade, Japanese manufacturing capital stock per employee increased by 10.6 percent per year, compared to a mere 1.8 percent in the United States. Moreover, during the second half of the decade, the productivity of capital improved in Japan while it worsened in the United States. In consequence, the Japanese lead in the growth of labor productivity widened, from 2.2 times the U.S. rate in the first half of the 1960s to nearly 5.5 times during the second half (table 5–5).

Why did the growth of capital stock per employee as well as the growth of real output per unit of capital diverge widely between the United States and Japan during the second half of the 1960s? Although there were factors specific to each country, two major factors—the Vietnam war and the Bretton Woods system of fixed exchange rates—caused opposite impacts on the two countries. It is well known that the excess demand conditions created by war-related additional expenditures stimulated the expansion of both economies. However, for Japan, which was not directly involved in the war efforts, the improved capacity utilization and trade balance stimulated stepped-up investments in new productive facilities. Japanese exports, supported by the increasingly undervalued but fixed exchange rate, expanded by 18.0 percent per year in terms of U.S. dollars during the second half of the 1960s, compared to 17.1 percent per year in the preceding twelve years (1953-1965) after the Korean war. Japan's terms of trade, which declined in the first half of the 1960s, also turned to its favor in the second half. In consequence, the Japanese current account balance, which was in deficit by $270 million a year on average during the the the first half of the decade, shifted into surplus, averaging $1.2 billion a year in the second half. This allowed the Japanese economy to prolong an economic boom (lasting over four and a half years), which, following previous experience, should have been cut short by an eventual worsening of balance of payments.

Investment activity in the private sector accelerated sharply during that boom. As a ratio to GNP, private investments in plant and equipment rose to 18.8 percent on average during the second half of the 1960s, compared to an average of 16.8 percent in the preceding eleven years (1955-1965). However, because of the tightening labor market situation, the growth of nonagricultural employment continued to decelerate, resulting in a rapid increase of capital stock per employee. Structural changes in the manufacturing sectors also contributed to the increase in capital intensity. The sectors that recorded above-average growth rates in the expansion of productive capacity during the second half of the 1960s were machinery, steel, nonferrous metals, and chemicals. Except for machinery, those sectors were characterized by relatively high capital coefficients.[3]

Despite the sharp expansion in productive capacity, capacity utilization was maintained at a high rate because of accelerated growth in production caused by the rapid growth of domestic demand and exports. During the second half of the 1960s, manufacturing production in Japan increased by 15.8 percent per year, compared to 11.1 percent per year in the first half. In consequence, capital productivity improved despite an increase in the growth of capital stock per employee, resulting in a rapid growth of real output per employee in the private sector.

In contrast to such favorable developments in Japan, both the Vietnam war and the fixed exchange rate system eventually proved detrimental to productivity growth in the U.S. economy. Although both aggregate demand and real output expanded in the second half of the 1960s at a rate markedly higher than in the first half, the composition of demand was such that the proportion of GNP invested in producers' durable equipment increased only moderately, from 5.1 percent to 6.4 percent on average for the respective five-year periods. In addition, a large share of these investments may have been made in defense-related industries, which added to the problems of excess capacity when the war ended. In the meantime, nearly 4 million men, one-fourth of all males in civilian population, in the twenty to twenty-nine age bracket were drawn into the Vietnam war between 1965 and 1970.[4] While their initial exit from the schools and civilian labor force made it easier for increased female participation (its participation rate increased 4 percentage points in the second half of the 1960s after gaining 1.6 percentage points during the first half), their reentry into the labor force in 1969–1970 coincided with a downturn in the economy, adding difficulties to the employment situation.

The adverse impact of the Vietnam war was exacerbated further by the fixed exchange rate under the Bretton Woods system, which caused a disequilibrium in the trade balances between the United States and its trade partners to persist longer than would have been the case under a more flexible exchange rate system. Until the imposition of a 10 percent import surcharge by President Nixon in August 1971 and the abandonment of the fixed exchange rate system in February 1973, a growing trade surplus allowed the Japanese economy to expand without the balance-of-payments constraint for the first time in its postwar history. It allowed the Japanese industries to expand and revamp their productive facilities, thereby further strengthening their export competitive position. Meanwhile, U.S. industries were deprived of whatever relief would have been afforded by a depreciating currency, and this may have retarded replacement investment in domestic productive facilities in sectors experiencing strong foreign competition, such as steel products and consumer electronics. Instead many of these industries felt compelled to relocate overseas the more labor-intensive parts of their operations in order to maintain overall profitability.[5] Those that could not do so (such as steel) failed to regain their vitality and continued to suffer decline.

The currency realignments between 1971 and 1973 and the imposition of wage-price controls in August 1971 provided much-needed relief to U.S. industries. Between 1970 and 1973, the rate of increase in employee compensation was contained at a rate slightly lower than the average in the preceding five years, while the growth of real output per employee in the manufacturing sector jumped to 4.3 percent per year between 1969 and 1973 from 2.3 percent per year in the preceding four years. The resulting decline in the rate of increase of unit labor costs apparently contributed to the improvement of investment climate in the United States. Between 1970 and

1973, U.S. private investment in producers' equipment increased by 9.1 percent per year in real terms, more than double the rate of the preceding five years. The resulting increase in capital intensity, combined with an improvement in capital productivity facilitated by a strong recovery in both export and domestic demands, helped to turn around the decline in the growth of labor productivity.

By contrast, in Japan during the same period, the growth of labor productivity suffered a reversal, and the rate of increase in unit labor costs accelerated sharply. Between 1970 and 1973, manufacturing output per employee increased by only 8.5 percent per year, compared to 12.5 percent per year in the preceding five years. The growth of export volume, partially dampened by a sharply appreciated yen, slowed down to 10.4 percent per year (from 15.5 percent per year in the preceding five years), and this contributed to a marked decline in the rate of capacity utilization as the large expansion in capital investment made in the late 1960s came on-stream. Meanwhile, a tightened labor market and a continued rise in the cost of living forced the steady upward adjustment of nominal wages in excess of the average rate in the preceding five years. As a result, manufacturing unit labor costs rose 8.7 percent per year between 1970 and 1973, more than four times the average rate of the preceding five years.

These unfavorable developments—the sharply upvalued yen, the decline in capacity utilization, and the extraordinary upsurge in unit labor costs— led the Japanese business sector to curtail its investment programs sharply in 1971–1972. However, during those two years Japan's current account balance registered a massive surplus of nearly $13 billion partly because of the J curve effect and partly because of improvements in services balance, caused by anticipations of further yen upvaluation. In this situation the Japanese authorities felt compelled to intervene heavily in the exchange markets to restrain the appreciation of the yen, in the process causing a strong expansion of bank credits. For three years from 1971 to 1973, the Japanese money supply expanded by 25 percent per year, on average, compared to 16.3 percent per year in the preceding three years. The Japanese government also sharply boosted fiscal expenditures and announced an ambitious plan to develop Japan's backward regions and to relieve its urban congestion and industrial concentration. In 1971 and 1972 Japanese fiscal expenditures as a percentage of GNP expanded markedly; in fact, the percentage continued to expand throughout the rest of the 1970s without much interruption (see figure 3–7).

These expansionary policies, in the presence of a worldwide economic boom, finally stimulated a sharp recovery in capital investment in 1973, which then lasted into 1974 despite a reversal of monetary policy—a response to upsurging inflation and quantum jumps in the price of oil. Inclusive of 1973, however, Japanese private investment in productive facilities increased by only 5.6 percent per year between 1971 and 1973, compared to over 22 percent per year in the preceding five years. This resulted in a sharp reversal in the growth of incremental capital per employee, although the growth of capital stock per employee was maintained because of maturation of investments made earlier. In any case, the productivity of capital declined markedly, thereby reducing the rate of growth of real output per employee.

After the Oil Shocks

The mutually feeding worldwide economic boom of 1972–1973 stimulated an expansion of investment demand that lasted into 1974; however, supply shortages for certain commodities and overall excess demand conditions gave rise to widespread upsurges in commodity prices and factor cost inflation, thus compelling the major industrial countries to tighten monetary policy even before the outbreak of the oil shock. In the ensuing recession among the industrial economies, the growth of real domestic demand in the seven years ended 1980 slackened to less than one-half (45 percent) of the rate in the preceding decade, although the extent of deceleration in demand growth varied widely among countries. In the United States the growth of real domestic demand was sustained at a relatively high rate compared to its historical records—an annual average rate of 2.3 percent for the period 1974–1980, or 55 percent of the rate in the preceding decade. Japan suffered one of the sharpest declines. The growth of real domestic demand during the same seven-year period fell to 3.4 percent per year—one-third of the rate in the preceding decade. The sharp deceleration in demand growth, offset only partially by an acceleration of export growth to the oil-exporting countries, resulted in the underutilization of both productive capacity and labor, discouraging private investment.

For the United States, whose dependence on imported oil was much less significant than Japan's and whose adjustment to the increased real price of oil was much slower because of continued controls on wellhead prices of domestically produced crude oil, the recovery of capacity utilization in the manufacturing sector was fairly swift, with the Federal Reserve series averaging 79.5 percent in 1976 compared to the recent peak annual rate of 87.6 percent in 1973. Since then, it has gradually increased, reaching 85.7 percent in 1979. In comparison, the recovery of capacity utilization in Japan was painfully slow. For Japan, whose postwar economic expansion was built on an abundant supply of relatively cheap fuels and raw materials, the need for adjustment was much greater because much of the nation's industrial capacity was biased toward intensive uses of these fuels and materials. Export growth was sustained at a high rate, considering the slowdown in the growth of world import demand; however, many sectors of

Japanese industries (particularly shipbuilding, steel, nonferrous metals, fibers, petrochemicals, and cement) were still depressed six years after the first oil shock, with the rate of capacity utilization in 1979 at 20 to 30 percent below their respective 1973 peaks. In aggregate, the index of manufacturing capacity utilization (excluding shipbuilding) was only 119 in 1979 compared to a 1973 peak of 128 and the 1975 trough of 100 (figure 5-4).

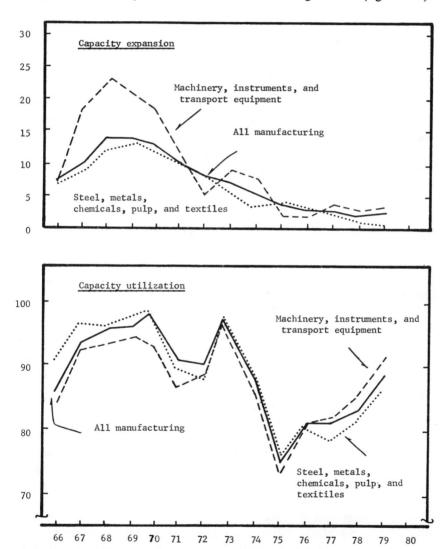

Figure 5-4. Expansion and Utilization of Productive Capacity in Japanese Manufacturing, 1966–1979 (percentages)

During this period, the growth of private investment in productive equipment declined sharply in both countries, though it was better sustained in the United States than in Japan. For the United States, private investment in producers' equipment increased at 2.8 percent per year in real terms between 1973 and 1980, compared to 9.1 percent per year between 1971 and 1973. For Japan, the average rate of growth, inclusive of the sharp recovery in 1979, was only 1.8 percent per year from 1974 to 1980. However, because of continued growth of civilian employment in the United States at a rate much higher than in Japan (3.0 percent annually versus 1.2), the growth of capital stock per employee declined sharply in both countries during the second half of the 1970s. In the United States it fell to 1.8 percent per year in manufacturing and to only 0.6 percent per year in the business sector, compared to 4.5 percent and 5.0 percent, respectively, for Japan. In consequence, the growth of real output per employee fell off sharply for both, except in Japan's manufacturing sector where productivity growth was maintained at a very high rate through a strong showing in capital productivity (table 5–5).

Why was Japan able to improve capital productivity despite a slow recovery in the rate of capacity utilization? The process of adjustment and consolidation in the Japanese manufacturing industries in the post-oil shock period involved important changes in the composition of new capital investment, output, and exports. Since the late 1960s, industries emphasizing skills and high technologies (such as automotive and electronic products) have gained shares at the expense of textiles and other industries producing traditional labor-intensive products, as well as steel, primary metals, and chemicals, which are products of heavy engineering processes. Except for a brief interruption in 1974–1975 caused by relative price changes in favor of oil and oil-based products, this trend resumed in the second half of the 1970s. One important contributing factor has been the change in relative cost position between the less energy-intensive machinery and instrument industries and the more energy-intensive steel and nonferrous metal industries. By 1979, various categories of machinery and instruments accounted for over 61 percent of Japan's merchandise exports, against 46 percent in 1970. This gain is even more impressive when the depressed exports of ships are excluded. The market share of traditional labor-intensive products suffered the greatest decline (50 percent), but the decline in the export share of steel and petrochemicals was even more pronounced in the second half of the 1970s (table 5–6). In recent years these shifts in demand and export competitive position have been reflected in the faster expansion of productive capacity and improvement in the rate of capacity utilization experienced by machinery and instrument industries. Despite a much faster capacity expansion beginning in 1977, the rate of capacity utilization rose faster for the machinery and instrument industries than for industries producing steel, nonferrous metals, chemicals, fibers, and paper and pulp (figure 5–4).

Table 5–6
Changes in Japanese Export Composition by Major Categories of Products, 1970–1979
(percentage of total)

	1970	1973	1975	1979
Steel, primary metals, and chemicals	28.0	25.8	30.8	25.2
Machinery and instruments	46.3	55.1	53.8	61.3
Ships	7.3	10.3	10.8	3.8
Other	39.0	44.8	43.0	57.5
Textiles	12.5	8.9	6.7	4.8
All other	13.2	10.2	8.7	8.7
Total	100.0	100.0	100.0	100.0

Source: Ministry of International Trade and Industry, *Tsusho Hakusho: Soron, 1980* (White paper on international trade, part I) (Tokyo: MITI, 1980), pp. 300–301.

Technology

Along with rapid growth in capital stock per employee, there has been a rapid advancement in the average technological level of Japanese industries and a corresponding shrinkage of the technological gaps that existed at the end of World War II between Japanese and U.S. firms. The lower the average age of the capital stock, the more efficient or productive it will be because of the embodiment of new technologies. During the period of rapid investment growth in the 1960s, the average age of Japanese capital stock declined markedly while declining only moderately in the United States. According to data collected by official Japanese sources, the average age of such stock declined from about eight years at the beginning of the 1960s to less than six years at the end of the decade. During the same period, the average age of American stock declined by about one year to about ten years in the early 1970s. Since then, however, the declining trend in Japan has been reversed (figure 5–5).

Under the impact of a protracted recession in the second half of the 1970s, investment in new productive capacities has shrunk in many industries as capacity utilization has remained low and corporate profit margins depressed. Except for selective industries (such as automobiles and electronic products) that maintained export competitiveness, whatever investment that continued was devoted mainly to maintenance and replacement, consolidation of excess capacities, and energy conservation. In consequence, the average age of Japanese capital stock increased to about 7.5 years in 1979, while that of the United States declined somewhat to 9.7 years.

Another indication of the catching up in technological levels was provided by self-assessment of the situation by Japanese business firms. Of the

Years

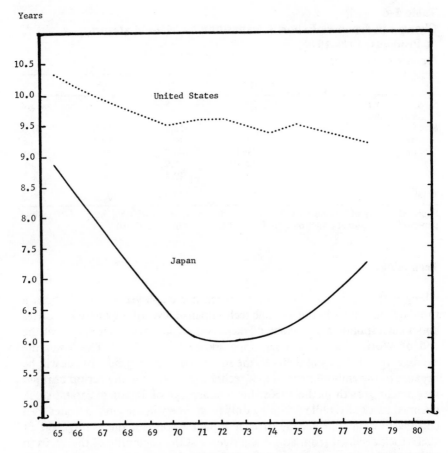

Figure 5–5. Average Age of Capital Stock in Manufacturing, 1965–1978

627 firms that responded to the queries by the Japanese Economic Planning Agency in January 1982, over one-third (36.2 percent) considered their technological levels to be above those of their competitors in the United States and Europe, and nearly one-half (44.6 percent) considered their technological levels to be at par with their foreign competitors, leaving only one-sixth or one-seventh lagging behind their overseas competitors. Companies with the more advanced technological levels expressed more confidence in their export competitiveness than did those lagging in technological advancements (table 5–7).

   The high proportion (at least four-fifths) of the sample firms that considered their technological levels to be at least at par with their foreign competitors underscores both the rapidity with which the Japanese firms have

Table 5-7

Japanese Manufacturing Firms' Own Evaluation of Technological Levels and Export Competitiveness Compared with Counterparts in the United States and Europe, January 1982

(percentage of total number of firms responding)

	Technological Levels Compared with Competitors in United States and Europe				
	Most Advanced	More Advanced	At Par	Lagging Behind	Lagging Far Behind[a]
International competitiveness					
Strong	25.7	5.4	12.0	6.2	0.8	1.3
Average	32.4	1.1	10.2	15.9	2.7	2.4
Weak	41.9	1.9	5.6	22.5	6.0	6.0
Total	100.0	8.4	27.8	44.6	9.5	9.7

Source: Result of a sampling survey with respect to business activity conducted by the Economic Planning Agency in January 1982 and reported in the agency's *Business Strategies for New Efficient Management and Development of Technologies* (Atarashii Koritsu Keiei to Gijutsu Kaihatsu ni Chosen suru Kigyo Keiei) (Tokyo, 1982).
Total number of firms responding was 627.
[a]Including "unknown."

caught up with the West and the changing role that they will play in the future. In the past, the success of Japanese exports has been based on so-called improvement engineering. By licensing the latest technologies developed elsewhere, improving on them, and making the finished goods better or cheaper than where they originally came from, many Japanese firms have been able to make world markets an extension of their domestic markets and thereby to improve further their operating efficiency.[6] However, as Japanese industries catch up to the West, increasingly they will have to play the role of technological innovator instead of technological imitator.

Will Japanese industrialists and technicians be comfortable with this change of role? In order to be successful, such a role reversal will require a sharp boost in R&D outlays and much more risk taking. More important, innovation can best thrive in a social environment that encourages personal initiative and bold individual actions. This is at odds with the conventional mode in Japan, which frowns on conspicuous individuality and favors consensual decision making and group action. This is a great challenge to the Japanese people. Deprived of the advantage of an undervalued exchange rate, an unlimited supply of cheap fuels, and once seemingly unlimited world markets, Japan must now search for a new pattern of technological development and economic growth. Inevitably such a pattern will have to be based more on the satisfaction of domestic needs as well as the development of new export industries using fewer imported raw materials but more sophisticated technology. So far, Japan seems to have coped with the changed world environment very well, as reflected in the moderation of wage behavior, the changing industrial structure favoring machinery and instruments, and marked progress toward reducing energy input per unit of national output. As the rapid development of industrial robots suggests, a slower growth in labor supply is not a serious constraint, it might even be a disguised blessing.[7] And the spirit of teamwork may even turn out to be conducive to the development of new technologies and products requiring heavy capital outlay and the close collaboration of many people—from technology development to product marketing. What appears to be still wanting is the realization that world markets are not unlimited unless there is a counterflow of capital and aid. Despite the so-called Nixon shock, the repeated oil shocks, and perennial trade problems with the United States and its East Asian neighbors because of its structural trade surplus, Japan has yet to develop the political leadership expected of a great economic power.[8]

U.S. industries have long played the role of technological leaders; however, as these industries have matured, established firms have tended to settle down to defensive positions. This is particularly so for many U.S. firms that were not dependent on export markets to attain economies of scale. Rather than scrap and rebuild, established firms tend to engage in cosmetic changes here and there as long as there is no major change in the underlying cost-price relationship.

This appears to have been the case for some of the declining industries (steel, textiles, automobile, and consumer electronic products) in the United States. These industries all share the common characteristic of being relatively labor intensive.[9] As inflation accelerated and labor markets tightened in the second half of the 1960s, these industries became particularly vulnerble to cost-push by labor unions and increased competition from the technological latecomers with lower wage costs. In fact, the wage level in the steel and automobile industries relative to the manufacturing average has long been higher in the United States than in Japan and Europe.[10] Since the latter part of the 1960s, there has been a further deterioration in these industries' relative cost position as their wage adjustment kept up with the industrial average while the growth of labor productivity suffered (table 5-8). Over time, the deterioration in the relative cost position of these industries tended to be reflected in the valuation of their assets in financial markets, and this made it even more difficult for them to obtain the necessary financing to replace outdated capital equipment and technologies. The resulting vicious circle tended to perpetuate the decline in competitive position of these industries.

The issue, then, is what to do with declining industries. Should the government raise import barriers to protect declining industries, or should it

Table 5-8

U.S. Steel Industry: Wage Rate and Unit Labor Costs in Relation to U.S. Manufacturing and Japanese Steel Industry, 1965-1978

	Wage Rate: Relative to U.S. Manufacturing (= 100)	Unit Labor Costs: Relative to	
		U.S. Manufacturing	Japanese Steel Industry[a]
1965	131	100	100
1970	124	102	122
1975	142	115	117
1978	155	116	131

Sources: U.S. data: Department of Labor, *Handbook of Labor Statistics* (December 1980); Department of Commerce, *Statistical Abstract of the United States* (various issues). Japanese data: *Rodo Tokei Yoran* (Handbook of labor statistics) (1982).

[a]Abstracted from changes in the exchange rate.

promote resource transfer out of them? One is struck by the difference in approach taken by the two governments with respect to industrial policy in general and declining industries in particular. The Japanese government has played an active role in formulating the nation's development plans and in promoting the development of new strategic industries. In contrast, the U.S. government plays a passive role in the promotion of industry, except where national defense is concerned. Another exception is the long-standing government leadership in agricultural research and development. In fact, there is no central organization for formulating industrial policy in the United States. In consequence, policies with respect to industrial development and international trade tend to be made by various government agencies on an ad hoc basis and without close coordination.[11] Thus the problems of declining industries are not considered in the context of promoting structural change and resource reallocation as in Japan. Over the years, trade barriers mainly in the form of so-called voluntary trade agreements have been set up to restrict the import of various products (such as cotton textiles, canned mushrooms, shoes, steel, and automobiles) that had become uncompetitive, but no adequate efforts were made to promote resource transfer and to retrain labor. Thus the problems of declining industries persist and constitute a major drag to the improvement of industrial efficiency. The backward-looking character of the U.S. approach with respect to declining industries provides a sharp contrast to the situation in Japan where the government provides financial aid to officially designated structurally depressed industries (such as aluminum refineries, synthetic fibers, shipbuilding, and open hearth and electric furnaces) for the specific purpose of scrapping excess capacities.[12]

In an open world economy, it is not difficult to determine which policy approach has been more effective. The positive, forward-looking Japanese approach has helped its industries to maintain cost competitiveness, thereby contributing to price stabilization. The passive, backward-looking U.S. policy has helped to perpetuate the unending vicious circle between cost-of-living increases and wage-price inflation.

Worker Motivation

In addition to faster investment growth and the economic advantage of being a technological latecomer, productivity growth in Japan has also benefited from the high motivation of its work force, a result of several factors, including the lifetime employment system. Several aspects of the Japanese system warrant attention.

Many Japanese products are reputed to have better quality and a much lower defect ratio than comparable U.S. products. For instance, it has been estimated that color television sets manufactured in Japan in 1979 had a defect ratio of 0.5 percent compared to 5 percent for comparable U.S. sets.[13] A high defect or recall ratio can spell disaster for corporate costs or profits. Why should Japanese products have such lower defect ratios in comparison to American products? It must be because the Japanese work force is better motivated and more disciplined than its American counterpart. It has been said that Japanese workers will stop the assembly line to install a missing part, while American workers would feign ignorance of the problem.[14]

One basic reason why the Japanese work force has been more motivated than its U.S. counterpart might be that the Japanese people were generally in accord with the system and institutions that made possible the rapid economic growth in the postwar decades. There might have been minor defects here and there, such as negative interest rates for financial savings, creeping consumer price inflation in the 1960s and much of the 1970s, and crowded living conditions in major cities, but the people were generally not too discontented so long as there were rapid income growth, ample employment opportunities, and a reasonably equitable income distribution system. There were no major domestic issues to polarize the population, and the people were not called to make major sacrifices as in the 1930s. In consequence, the social order was maintained, and the authorities were respected. The great majority of the population was willing to work within the system.[15]

In contrast, American youth were conscripted to fight two major wars without clearly defined enemies and without really winning the wars. Many other domestic issues pitched one segment of the population against another, including the civil rights movement, the busing of school children, and student protest against the Vietnam war. The corruption of power in high office, including the Watergate affair in the early 1970s, made many youths cynical of the political process and distrustful of the authorities. A heterogeneous racial composition and a modest economic growth rate combined with a labor force growth rate far above historical patterns made high unemployment inevitable for the bulging youth labor force in times of economic downturns. The neglect and decay of the inner cities posed a stark contrast to the affluent suburbs, and the failure of the authorities to rectify the system tended to induce the discontented to take authority into their own hands at slight pretext, as manifest in massive break-ins of private properties during electrical blackouts in New York City. Under such conditions, it is no wonder that many workers did not care whether the cars they were assembling missed a few parts.

Under the Japanese system, young people, rich or poor, undergo intense competition to enter the most desirable universities. After graduation from top schools, they are recruited by powerful cabinet ministries or the large, renowned corporations. There they go up the career ladder step by step, and retire around age fifty-five (now extended to around age sixty-one) to have a second career, such as going into politics, starting a small business, joining a company in an advisory capacity, or becoming a full-time college professor. Most recruitments are for new graduates, and there is little opportunity for a change of career in midstream. Once joining an organization, new employees are expected to stay and are given a series of on-the-job training and rotation of jobs to gain experience. Promotions are orderly and above board. Competition for promotions exists only between colleagues who joined the organization in the same year. No employee is allowed to linger in the coveted posts for too long or suffer the shame of being bypassed for promotion by younger colleagues.

Under this system, seniority is respected, and it serves as the cornerstone of stability both within the organization and for society in general. The authorities are respected because competition is fair and promotion orderly. The system runs smoothly, and whatever microinefficiencies that may exist are overwhelmed by macroefficiency. The system works, helped by a public sector that is small and lean and because rapid economic growth creates plenty of opportunities for those disinclined to a bureaucratic or professional way of life.

The Japanese system is conducive to productivity growth for several reasons. More individuals are dedicated to their work because competition is fair and promotion orderly. Except for education prior to joining an organization, both the cost and benefit of training are internalized within the organization.[16] Individuals continue to grow after joining an organization because they are given plenty of training and work experiences. Individuals do not feel threatened by the implementation of more efficient work methods, equipment, or processes because employment is assured until retirement, and those innovations can only make their work easier or less tedious. In fact, employees are motivated to suggest innovations within the work place.

In comparison, the U.S. system is less conducive to productivity growth for several reasons. Fewer individuals are dedicated to their work because they no longer believe the system is working. Work becomes a chore or at best a way of earning a living. Jobs are transient, particularly at the non-professional level. Even at the professional level, switching of jobs is frequent, and there is no commitment to one's job. Individuals are employed for what they are worth now, not for their potential. Except for a selected few, they are not trained or given wide experience within the same organization. In consequence, most individuals do not grow on the job. They are treated as specialists, whose effectiveness may decrease over time because of rapid obsolescence of knowledge or skills acquired earlier. Individuals are threatened by replacement by improved work methods, equipment, or processes. In consequence, they are opposed to the introduction of such innovations.[17] Since individuals are powerless, opposition takes the form of confrontation between the union and management, resulting in frequent strikes (table 5-9). The high defect ratio due to low morale and frequent work stoppages due to management-worker disputes are both inimical to productivity growth.

Table 5-9
Number of Workdays Lost Due to Labor Disputes, 1965-1980
(1,000 days)

	Japan	West Germany	United States	United Kingdom
1965	5,669	49	23,300	2,925
1966	2,742	27	25,400	2,398
1967	1,830	390	42,100	2,787
1968	2,814	25	49,018	4,690
1969	3,634	249	42,869	6,346
1970	3,915	93	66,414	10,980
1971	6,029	2,599	47,589	13,551
1972	5,147	66	27,066	23,909
1973	4,604	563	27,948	7,197
1974	9,663	1,051	47,991	14,750
1975	-8,016	69	31,237	6,012
1976	3,254	534	37,859	3,284
1977	1,518	24	35,822	10,142
1978	1,358	4,281	37,000	9,405
1979	930	483	33,000	29,474
1980	1,001	128	32,000	11,964

Source: Bank of Japan: *Kokusai Hikaku Tokei* (Comparative international statistics) (June 1982); and *Gaikoku Keizai Tokei Nenpo* (Foreign economic statistical annual, 1980) (October 1981).

Notes

1. Measurement of productivity growth in the government sector and personal services is a controversial subject. Under the present national income accounting convention, productivity of government employees may rise only if there is an increase in complementary inputs per employee. In the rest of this chapter, comparison is made only of private sector productivity.

2. The Japanese capital stock was converted into the U.S. dollar equivalent at the rate of 305 yen per dollar.

3. Cement and rubber products recorded a rate of capacity expansion slightly below average, while the rate of capacity expansion for textiles and paper and pulp was only 5 to 7 percent per year compared to the 12.2 percent per year average.

4. See Elizabeth Waldman, "Vietnam War Veterans—Transition to Civilian Life," *Monthly Labor Review* (November 1970).

5. For specific corporate examples, see Jack Baranson, *The Japanese Challenge to U.S. Industry* (Lexington, Mass.: Lexington Books, D.C. Heath and Company, 1981), chaps. 6, 7.

6. This Japanese knack for improvement engineering, although best symbolized by consumer electronic products (such as Sony television sets), is not limited to manufacturing but prevails in many other activities, including music and sports. In fact, this is not the first time in Japanese history Japan has succeeded in doing this on a grand scale. In the seventh century, it successfully absorbed classical Chinese culture, modifying it to suit Japanese tastes, and made Japan the home of, for example, the best chinaware, or zen, a Buddhist cult.

7. Japan now leads the world in the production and use of industrial robots. According to the Robot Institute of America, nearly 60 percent of programmable robots in use worldwide are found in Japan.

8. One avenue for Japan to maintain its heavy industrial base is to export plant and equipment to the People's Republic of China on a large scale for ten to fifteen years by granting concessionary credit of the IDA (International Development Association) type. Such an arrangement would be logical considering Japan's proximity to China and its heavy involvement there before the end of World War II. This will require a basic restructuring of Japan's foreign aid policy.

9. Even the capital-labor ratio for the steel industry did not exceed the manufacturing average because of its lag in rebuilding productive facilities. See Robert W. Randall, *The U.S. Steel Industry in Recurrent Crisis: Policy Options in a Competitive World* (Washington, D.C.: Brookings, 1981), p. 33.

10. Ibid., p. 35.

11. See, for example, Robert B. Reich, "Making Industrial Policy," *Foreign Affairs* (Spring 1982).

12. See Gary R. Saxonhouse, "Industrial Restructuring in Japan," *Journal of Japanese Studies* 5 (Summer 1979):305-321, and Ira C. Magaziner and Thomas M. Hout, *Japanese Industrial Policy* (Berkeley: Institute of International Studies, University of California: Policy Papers in International Affairs, 1980), pp. 30-87.

13. Baranson, *Japanese Challenge,* p. 180.

14. Adam Smith [pseud.], *Super-Money* (New York: Popular Library, 1972), pp. 238-239.

15. This is a far cry from the situation in the decade preceding Japan's invasion of Manchuria when the country was beset by widespread social discontent and unrest. The humiliation of a major defeat, combined with institutional reforms instituted after World War II (including the equalization of agricultural landownership and legalization of labor unions), apparently contributed to the restoration of social cohesiveness in Japan.

16. Although undergraduate education in the social sciences and humanities in U.S. universities seems more vigorous and disciplined than its counterpart in Japan, the latter has a long tradition of emphasizing vocational training at the high school level for students not going to college. In comparison, U.S. educational facilities for vocational training are spotty at best. Although this is only a personal observation, it appears that Japanese blue-collar workers are better educated and trained than their American counterparts.

17. Thus, automakers cannot cut production costs through increased subcontracting. In the Japanese system, subcontracting is freely used as a means, among others, to meet cyclical changes in business volumes.

6

Government's Role in the Financial Intermediation of Saving and Investment

Differences in saving and investment behavior represent another aspect of the divergence in economic performance between the United States and Japan. These differences existed before, and persisted after, the oil shocks. During the twenty years prior to the first oil crisis, the high propensity of Japanese households to save provided a major source of funds for the business sector to finance a high rate of capital formation without much inflation. This was made possible through a system of financial intermediation and government guidance that had no equal in the United States. Since 1974, the personal savings ratio in Japan has remained at a rather high level, though there has been a slight decline in the more recent past, and this has enabled the government to expand greatly its fiscal deficit, through bond issues, without seriously aggravating inflation.

In contrast, despite a higher per-capita income, the U.S. personal savings ratio has averaged only about three-fifths of that of Japan during most of the postwar decades. In recent years, this ratio has even suffered an appreciable decline. During the second half of the 1970s, the size of the U.S. fiscal deficit, though large in absolute amount, was much smaller than that in Japan in relation to GNP. Yet the expansion of fiscal deficit has been perennially perceived as an inflationary threat in the United States.

These differences in economic behavior, partly functional and partly institutional, give rise to a number of questions. The first concerns the wide disparity in personal saving behavior. In particular, why is the Japanese households' propensity to save so strong compared to that of their U.S. counterparts despite their relatively low per-capita income, and why was the former's saving propensity seemingly less affected by the first oil shock compared to the American experience? Second, how or why was excess household savings in Japan channeled, in large measure, to productive investment prior to the first oil shock? Such savings went to more diversified outlets (such as Treasury bills and other financial instruments) in the United States. Third, what was the role of government in causing such divergent investment patterns? What were the key differences in the respective financial systems that produced these investment outcomes? The last question concerns the manner in which fiscal deficits were financed. In particular, why have the smaller U.S. deficits (in relation to GNP) been perceived as a major inflationary threat, while the much larger Japanese deficits (similarly defined) so far have not caused significant inflationary movements? These questions are examined in this chapter.

Changing Sources and Uses of Domestic Savings

Throughout the 1960s and early 1970s, the Japanese people saved and invested over one-third (about 36 percent) of their GNP. In comparison, the American people saved and invested only about one-fifth of their GNP.[1] The Japanese savings ratio had been increasing steadily over time, from around 20 percent in the early 1950s to about 40 percent in the early 1970s. The U.S. ratio has changed little over time. In the aftermath of the first oil shock, the aggregate savings ratio of both countries suffered a decline, although the decline was steeper in Japan than in the United States. In Japan, it declined from some 40 percent in 1971–1973 to 36 percent in 1974–1975, and to 32 percent in 1976–1978. In comparison, the U.S. ratio declined only slightly from 19 percent in 1971–1973 to 18.5 percent in 1976–1978. After the second oil shock, both countries appeared to have suffered a further decline in the gross domestic saving ratio (figure 6–1 and table 6–1).[2]

Before the onslaught of the first oil shock, over two-fifths of Japan's gross domestic savings was accounted for by the business sector, which includes both private and public enterprises. The household sector provided less than two-fifths and the general government less than one-fifth. However, whereas the savings ratio of the household sector continued to rise through the 1960s and 1970s, that of the business sector fell sharply during the 1970s after reaching a peak at the end of the 1960s (figure 6–2). In comparison, the general government's savings ratio continued to rise through the first half of the 1970s before falling off markedly in the second half. Most conspicuous was the contrast in saving behavior between the household and the business sectors in the aftermath of the first oil shock. While the household sector's gross savings rose from 16 percent of GNP in 1971–1973 to more than 20 percent in 1974–1978, those of the business sectors declined by 6 to 7 percentage points to 9 to 10 percent of GNP during the same period. Excluding provisions for capital consumption, the business sectors dissaved in 1974–1975 and made little net saving during 1976–1978. The poor performance of business savings after the first oil shock occurred in conjunction with a protracted recession and sluggish economic growth experienced by the Japanese economy. Reflecting the improvements of business conditions since 1979, net business savings remained positive after the second oil shock, but household savings suffered a further decline.

In comparison, U.S. household savings, while being only three-fifths of the Japanese level as a percentage of GNP, accounted for 45 percent to

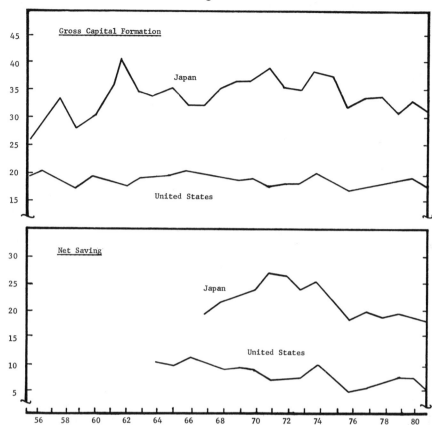

Figure 6–1. Evolution of Gross Capital Formation and Net Saving in Relation to GNP, 1955–1980 (percentages)

nearly one-half of gross domestic savings in the United States in the years prior to the first oil shock. The business sector provided two-fifths, the government slightly over one-tenth. In contrast with the rising trend in Japan, household savings in the United States changed little over time in relation to GNP. Since 1976, however, the U.S. household savings ratio suffered a decline of 1 to 2 percentage points despite a recovery in economic activity from the 1974–1975 recession. The business savings ratio, which amounted to less than one-half of the Japanese ratio before the first oil shock, changed relatively little over time, except for a moderate weakening in net savings since 1974 (figure 6–2). The government savings, which amounted to about one-third of the Japanese ratio during the 1960s and early 1970s, turned sharply negative in 1975–1976, excluding provisions for capital consumption.

Table 6-1
Sectoral Balance on Saving and Investment, 1966–1980
(percentage of GDP)

	Household[a]			Business[b]			General Government[c]			Rest of the World[d]
	Saving	Investment	Balance	Saving	Investment	Balance	Saving	Investment	Balance	
United States										
1966–1970	8.7	6.0	2.7	8.2	10.0	−1.8	2.7	2.8	−0.1	−0.8
1971–1973	9.3	7.3	2.0	7.9	9.8	−1.9	1.8	2.3	−.5	.4
1974–1975	10.3	5.8	4.5	8.1	9.8	−1.7	.4	2.3	−1.9	−.9
1976–1978	8.3	6.7	1.6	9.1	10.6	−1.5	1.1	1.9	−.8	.7
1979–1980	8.2			8.8			1.6			
Japan										
1966–1970	13.9	8.8	5.1	16.1	23.0	−6.9	6.2	4.4	1.8	.0
1971–1973	15.9	10.2	5.7	16.0	20.9	−4.9	7.9	5.4	2.4	−3.2
1974–1975	20.6	10.7	9.9	8.9	19.2	−10.3	5.2	5.3	−.1	.8
1976–1978	20.2	10.6	9.6	9.7	15.2	−5.5	2.4	5.7	−3.3	−.8
1979–1980	18.9	10.2	7.7	9.6	16.3	−6.7	3.2	6.4	−3.2	2.2

Source: Organisation for Economic Cooperation and Development, *National Accounts of OECD Countries, 1951–1980* (Paris: OECD, 1982).

Note: Includes consumption of fixed capital.

[a]Includes private nonprofit institutions serving households.

[b]Includes public enterprises.

[c]Includes all levels of governments, plus social security funds.

[d]Sum of domestic sectors, plus statistical discrepancy, with signs reversed.

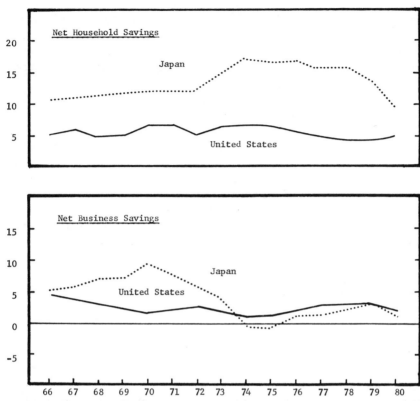

Figure 6-2. Evolution of Net Household Savings and Net Business Savings in Relation to GNP, 1966–1980 (percentages)

Until the first oil shock, the steady rise in Japan's private savings took place in conjunction with a similar rise in the ratio of gross investment in the private economy. This investment was concentrated in the business sector, which rose from about 11 percent of GNP in the early 1950s to about 25 percent in the early 1970s. Investment in the household sector also rose, from 6.5 percent of GNP to 10 percent, but the sector's excess savings nevertheless expanded, from 3 percent of GNP to 10.5 percent. Since the government sector remained in surplus because the tax revenue was highly income elastic, the increasing surplus in household savings provided a steadily expanding source of funds for private capital investment in the 1960s and an expanding balance-of-payments surplus in the eary 1970s.

Following the first oil crisis and the ensuing recession, business investment plummeted while the household savings ratio continued to rise. The former dropped by 6 percentage points from 1973 to 1978, after falling 4 percentage points from 1970 to 1973. Although the business sector's savings ratio also declined, its need for external financing nevertheless shrank. The resulting surplus in household savings was soaked up by the government through increased sales of bonds to financial institutions, to finance a larger public investment in relation to GNP.

In comparison, in the United States, a stable investment ratio, excluding cyclical fluctuations, accompanied a stable savings ratio in the private economy. Since the mid-1950s, private domestic investment has oscillated in a narrow band between 15 percent and 19 percent of GNP without displaying a clear trend. Even the marked fall in 1975, to 14.3 percent, was followed by a quick recovery to an average of 18.0 percent in 1977–1979; however, because of the decline of the government savings ratio since 1974, government deficit as a percentage of GNP increased in certain years and constituted a stronger competition to the business sector for the relatively small household surplus savings.

Factors behind Japan's High Savings Ratio

Why did the Japanese save and invest increasingly larger shares of their GNP while Americans did not? Since this has been a long-term development encompassing nearly a quarter-century, it is not meaningful to isolate the saving process from the investment process. If the investment ratio exceeded the savings ratio for an extended period of time, there had to be a mechanism, both economic and political, to accept increased foreign participation in the domestic economy. For better or worse, this apparently was not the case in Japan. On the other hand, if the savings ratio consistently exceeded the investment ratio, there had to be outlets for overseas investment or government policy for expanded foreign aid. This, again, was not the case in postwar Japan after the loss of its former colonies at the end of World War II.

On the contrary, there were strong inducements for rapid investment growth in Japan in the two decades prior to the onslaught of the oil shocks. These inducements included a strong need to catch up with the advanced countries in productive capacity and technology development, a favorable external environment that allowed Japan to pursue a pattern of economic growth based on increased exports of manufactures in exchange for necessary fuels and raw materials, and active government promotion. Japan started its postwar economic development from a level of per-capita income and capital stock that was only a small fraction of that of the United States; the development process, unless sidetracked by such major hindrances as the oil crisis and world economic depression, will not let up until a sense of maturity develops in the Japanese economy. This will occur when Japan has caught up with the world industrial leader, the United States, in terms of technological level and material welfare. Japanese industrial leaders are now more confident of their technological command and export competitive position, but Japan still falls far behind the United States in accumulation of per-capita capital stock, particularly in areas not directly related to industrial production.

In comparing long-term saving and investment behavior in Japan and America, there is one advantage on the part of the Japanese economy that cannot be ignored: The "Peace Constitution" and the American nuclear umbrella have saved Japan 5 to 10 percent of GNP (compared with the United States) for nondefense purposes, which Japan used wisely to equip its labor force with advanced capital equipment.[3] From the point of view of generating income and employment in the short run, the demand stimulative effect of 5 to 10 percent of GNP will probably not differ too much whether it was used for public consumption such as national defense or for investing in productive facilities. Over the long run, however, it must have caused a great disparity in the growth of per-capita capital stock and labor productivity.

Also important in this connection is the large difference in tax burden borne by individuals and corporations between the two countries. Based on national income data, taxes and nontax payments as a ratio to national income were at least 10 percent higher in the United States than in Japan during the 1970s. Moreover, the differential was much greater for corporate income tax than for individual income tax (table 6–2 and figure 6–3). A larger tax burden may affect adversely the economic agents' capacity to save, and

Table 6–2
Comparison of U.S. and Japanese Tax Burden, 1972 and 1978
(percentages)

	United States		Japan	
	1972	1978	1972	1978
Taxes and nontax payments/ national income	37.2	38.7	24.6	28.7
Individual income tax[a]/ personal income	19.9	21.5	11.8	13.1
Corporate income tax[a]/ corporate income	44.9	50.4	22.5	34.5
Indirect taxes/taxes and nontax payments	31.5	26.9	35.5	29.7
Fiscal expenditures/GNP	19.5	21.4	12.4	16.5

Source: Bank of Japan, *Kokusai Hikaku Tokei* (Comparative international statistics) (Tokyo, June 1982). Tax ratios are computed on the basis of national income data published by the OECD.

[a]Including other direct taxes and nontax payments.

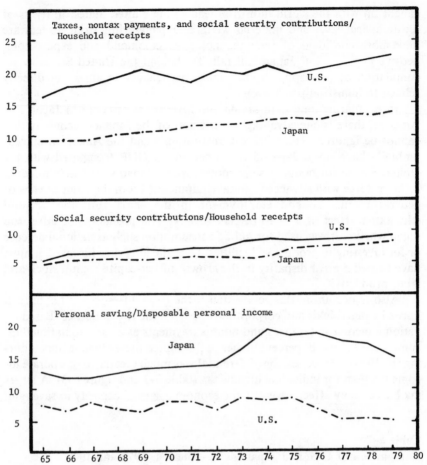

Figure 6-3. Ratio of Taxes and Social Security Contributions to Household
Receipts and Ratio of Personal Savings to Disposable Personal
Income, 1965–1980 (percentages)

it may result in a lower rate of capital formation than otherwise if a large
part of the higher tax revenues is used for nonproductive purposes such as
defense.

From a dynamic economic growth point of view, the more basic factor
for a rising saving ratio must be found in the virtuous circle between rapid
economic growth and industrialization on one hand and rising saving and
investment capacity on the other. As the growth of per-capita income accelerated, the capacity for saving was enhanced, enabling Japan to raise investment without relying on an extended inflow of foreign capital. In the

meantime, the growth of productive capital stock, the absorption of borrowed technologies, and the improvement in the quality of the labor force enabled Japan to help its export competitive position through the improvement of product quality, product innovation, and improvements in labor productivity. In turn, this enabled Japan to maintain a high rate of investment and income growth without a serious constraint on the balance of payments. Thus, until the termination of the Bretton Woods system of adjustable parities, the onslaught of the oil shocks, and the emergence of a prolonged world economic recession in the 1970s, Japan was able to take full advantage of a favorable external environment to attain a trend acceleration in its economic growth.[4]

During the process of rapid industrialization and economic growth, massive transfers of the labor force from the rural agricultural sector to the urban industrial and service sectors took place. The resulting urbanization of the population was accompanied by a decline in average family size. This process required massive reconstruction of various economic infrastructures as well as commercial and residential buildings. The limited availability of urban land, combined with an age-old Japanese preference for single-family housing, each with an enclosed yard, led to a persistent rise in the relative price of suitable building lots and in the amount of household savings required for purchasing or building each family's dream home.[5] The break-up of multigenerational households, the maintenance of the compulsory retirement system at around age fifty-five despite a significant extension in average life expectancy, combined with the late development of a national pension system, has encouraged wage earners to save an increasing share of current income for retirement.[6] In addition, a rapid increase in the proportion of high school graduates going to college, given the paucity of financial aid for education, has also forced the current generation of Japanese parents to save more for their children's education.

Hence, there were ample motivations for Japanese househlds to save a high, even rising, share of their current incomes. This process was facilitated by the widespread practice (for both white and blue-collar workers in businesses and government) of receiving wages and salaries in the form of large bonuses twice a year. Although the bonus system has become so entrenched that the ratio of special payments to regular wage bill changes little in response to cyclical fluctuations in aggregate economic activity (figure 6-4), it nevertheless provided a convenient mechanism for household savings, considering the late development of installment purchase plans, use of credit cards, and mortgage financing in Japan. In fact, this mechanism may explain the slow decline in household savings ratio in 1974–1976 when wage earners may have grown cautious in their spending patterns because of a worsening business and employment situation, resulting in additional saving out of their semiannual bonuses.

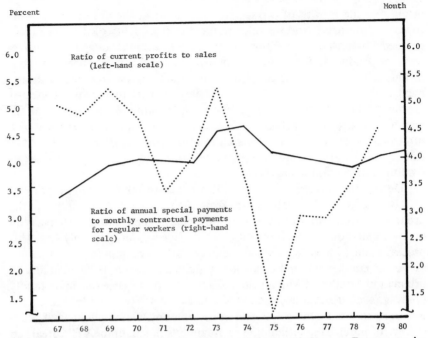

Figure 6-4. Japanese Profit Margins and Rate of Bonus Payments in Manufacturing Industries, 1967-1980

By contrast, social security and installment purchase plans have long been an established feature of American life. Also, the recovery in economic activity and employment after the sharp dip in 1975 was much swifter in the United States than in Japan. For these reasons, the impacts of the 1974-1975 disturbances on the propensity of U.S. households to spend may have been largely cyclical. Although the proportion of the population over sixty-five continued to increase from 1965 to 1980, this was offset by a decline in the proportion of those under twenty-one, so that there was actually an increase in the working age population.[7] Hence, changes in the age composition of the population may not have been a major cause of the appreciable decline in the personal saving ratio since 1976. Rather, both the slowdown in the growth of real income and changes in financial returns under persistent inflation may have caused a change in both the rate and pattern of household savings. First, low or negative real returns on financial investments discouraged investments in financial instruments. Second, rapid appreciation in the value of residential structures, combined with unlimited tax credits for mortgage interest payments, encouraged investment in owner-occupied or rental housing, particularly among two-worker middle-class families, whose number has been increasing. The widespread practice of installment purchases and mortgage financing also caused an increase in the proportion of disposable income devoted to essential goods and services, as well as to interest payments on home mortgage and other financial debts. These changes caused an increase in the share of savings kept in the form of real assets, which have appreciated but have not counted as an increase in income in the national income account while increasing household expenses or reducing measured savings in the national income account.[8]

Between 1965–1974 and 1977–1979, the increase in U.S. consumer financial liabilities, as a percentage of disposable personal income, far exceeded (by 2.5 percentage points) the increase in the households' acquisition of financial assets. During the same period, net purchases of owner-occupied housing increased, by 1.3 percent of disposable personal income, while the proportion devoted to net purchases of consumer durables slightly declined. Combined with the sharp rise in interest rates and energy costs, this has resulted in a marked increase in the proportion of U.S. households' disposable income devoted to payments for essential goods and services and financial charges. Between 1970–1974 and 1977–1979, the percentage of U.S. personal disposable income devoted to the payment of mortgages and other consumer debts increased by 3.9 percentage points, while interest payments for these debts also increased by 2.0 percentage points. During the same period, consumer outlays for essential goods and services increased by 2.0 percentage points, while their outlays for other goods and services declined by 1.2 percent.[9] In particular, the combined share of energy and food, which declined by over 6 percentage points from the late 1950s to the early 1970s, has increased by 3 percentage points since then. Whereas the decline in the 1960s was caused principally by a drop in the relative cost of food items and partially by that of energy products and services, the recent increase was due exclusively to a rise in the relative cost of energy.[10] As a result, the ratio of personal saving to personal disposable income suffered a marked decline, from 7.3 percent in 1970–1974 to 4.8 percent in 1977–1979.

Government Influences on the Financial Intermediation of Saving and Investment Activity

The high and rising investment ratio in Japan during the two decades prior to the first oil shock was encouraged by a process of financial intermediation in which policy guidance by government, particularly the Bank of Japan, played an important role. Such a process, which is distinct from that prevailing in the United States, was characterized by several features:

1. A rapid growth of investment activity by large corporations, concentrating in industrial sectors that are technologically advanced, structurally strategic, or export oriented. The mix of these industries may change from time to time, but it tended to include growing, rather than declining, industries.

2. The heavy dependence of these corporations on investment funds from commercial banks headquartered in three megalopolises. Smaller manufacturing firms engaged in export activity were dependent on larger trading firms for financing, but the latter dealt primarily with city banks.

3. City banks supplemented their sources of loanable funds by borrowing from the regional banks and the specialized banks through the interbank market and from the Bank of Japan through discounting, with commercial papers obtained from large corporations.

4. The large corporations tended to overborrow from the city banks instead of relying on internal funds or issuing corporate securities. This was because during the high-growth period, the generation of internal funds was not rapid enough to meet ever-increasing needs for expansion and because the issuing of corporate securities was not as expedient as borrowing from the banks since capital markets were underdeveloped and bank interest rates were kept low by the government.

5. City banks were almost perpetually in debt to the Bank of Japan since the latter's discount rate was much lower than the money market call rates. The city banks thus performed important functions in the mobilization and allocation of Japan's rapidly growing domestic savings. Not only were they in the center of financing investment needs of Japan's leading industrial sectors, but they also influenced the direction of investment activity by borrowing surplus funds from other sectors or financial institutions for relending to their favorite industrial clients. Also, by being continuously in debt to the Bank of Japan, they also served as an important medium for the latter's control of the rate of bank credit expansion and consequently of the rate of growth of investment activity in the major corporate sector at a time when the discounting of corporate papers was the principal means of controlling the rate of change in the money supply.[11]

Based on national account data, during the first half of the 1970s, some 70 percent of funds used by Japanese nonfarm nonfinancial corporations was externally financed, of which 40 percent was bank loans. By contrast, U.S. corporations were dependent on external sources for only one-half of their total funds and ony 10 percent in bank credits (table 6–3). During the same period, based on the Bank of Japan's flow of funds data, city banks in Japan accounted for, on average, 26.8 percent of outstanding loans and

Table 6–3
Sources of Funds for Nonfarm Nonfinancial Corporate Business, 1966–1980
(percentages)

	United States			Japan	
	1966–1970	*1971–1975*	*1976–1980*[a]	*1971–1975*	*1976–1980*
Internal funds	57.7	50.0	56.5	28.9	37.6
Provisions for capital consumption	44.2	42.7	41.1	25.3	32.5
Undistributed profits	13.5	9.3	13.3	3.6	5.1
External funds	42.3	50.0	43.4	71.1	62.3
Securities and mortgages	20.6	25.9	25.9	7.9	9.1
Bank loans	10.8	9.8	12.2	39.5	30.8
Trade credits	10.9	14.3	13.2	23.7	22.4

Sources: United States: Board of Governors of the Federal Reserve System, *Flow of Funds Accounts, 1949–1978* (December 1979), and Council of Economic Advisers, *Economic Indicators* (July 1981). Japan: Economic Planning Agency, *Annual Report on National Accounts, 1982.*
[a]Details do not round up to subtotal because they are based on data for 1976–1978.

investments made by all financial institutions. These loans and investments exceeded by 3.8 percentage points their share in deposits and other sources of funds. In contrast, the share of loans and investments accounted for by regional banks and other financial institutions (excluding public institutions) fell 4.5 percentage points short of their share in deposits and other sources of funds (table 6–4). During the same period, the city banks' borrowings from the Bank of Japan amounted to, on average, 5.6 percent of their combined liabilities and net worth, while the ratio was only 0.3 percent for regional banks (table 6–5).

This pattern of financial intermediation, with city banks in the vanguard and the nation's monetary and economic policymaking authorities providing the guiding lights, successfully channeled Japanese households' increasing excess savings to productive uses, thereby helping to foster a high rate of growth in investment and productive capacity (table 6–6).[12] The system was not without its critics, however. Because of the low interest rate policy pursued by the government and the formation of close client relationships between the banks and large corporations, borrowers tended to overborrow, and lenders tended to overlend, leading to excessive investments in fields that were then profitable while neglecting fields that were less profitable but nevertheless important. Thus was formed in Japan, a country without its own iron ore and crude oil, the world's highest proportion of steel and chemical industries in its industrial structure. Meanwhile, in spite of a stable or even declining wholesale price index in the 1960s, the consumer price index continued to increase because of inadequate investments in the service

Table 6-4
Japanese Distributions of Sources and Uses of Funds by City Banks and Other Financial Institutions, 1966-1979
(percentages)

	1966-1970	*1971-1974*	*1975-1979*
Uses of funds			
City banks	26.8	25.3	21.3
Other private banks and financial institutions	55.6	56.7	56.1
Public financial institutions	17.6	18.0	22.6
Sources of funds			
City banks	23.0	22.1	18.3
Other private banks and financial institutions	60.1	59.6	58.3
Public financial institutions	16.9	18.3	23.4
Excess of source over use			
City banks	−3.8	−3.2	−3.0
Other private banks and financial institutions	4.5	2.9	2.2
Public financial institutions	−.7	−.3	−.8

Source: Bank of Japan, *Flow of Funds Accounts* and Yoshio Suzuki, *Nihon Keizai to Kinyu: Sono Tenkan to Tekio* (Japanese economy and finance: Changes and adaptation) (Tokyo: Toyo Keizai Shimposha, 1981), pp. 246-247.

and distribution activity. This bias in the system apparently reached its extreme in the 1960s and the early 1970s when discipline against excessive investments broke down because of improvements in the balance of payments. Therefore, when the external environment worsened in 1974-1975, Japanese industries found themselves saddled with huge excess capacities, particularly

Table 6-5
Japanese Commercial Banks' Borrowing from Bank of Japan as a Percentage of Liabilities and Net Worth, 1966-1978

	Total Borrowed Money	*Borrowing from Bank of Japan*
1966-1970		
City banks	7.3	5.6
Regional banks	.4	.3
1971-1974		
City banks	3.6	3.1
Regional banks	.3	.2
1975-1978		
City banks	2.2	1.9
Regional banks	.3	.1

Source: Compiled from Bank of Japan, *Economic Statistical Annual* (1980), pp. 95-102.

Table 6–6

Composition of Financial Assets Held by Household Sector, 1970, 1975, and 1980

(percentages)

	United States			Japan		
	1970	*1975*	*1980*	*1970*	*1975*	*1980*
Currency and demand deposits	6.1	6.7	6.0	19.0	17.9	13.2
Savings deposits, etc.	22.1	30.1	28.8	46.5	57.3	60.8
Insurance and pension fund reserves	19.2	20.8	21.1	13.2	12.8	13.8
Corporate equities	37.9	25.8	27.1	6.5	3.1	2.0
Other securities	13.1	14.8	15.1	7.7	8.9	10.1
Total financial assets	100.0	100.0	100.0	100.0	100.0	100.0
Reference						
M1/GNP[a]	22.0	18.7	14.8	29.1	33.8	29.6
M2/GNP	63.8	66.1	63.6	73.8	91.5	88.1

Sources: Bank of Japan, *Kokusai Hikaku Tokei* (Comparative international statistics) (Tokyo, June 1982); Board of Governors, Federal Reserve System, *Flow of Funds Accounts, 1949–1978* (Washington, D.C., December 1979); and International Monetary Fund, *International Financial Statistics* (various issues).

[a]M1A for the United States.

in sectors heavily dependent on imported raw materials, such as heavy chemicals, steel and aluminum, as well as shipbuilding. Hence, by helping to create such an investment pattern and industrial structure, the system should also be held responsible, at least partially, for the length of Japan's industrial recession in the post-oil shock period.

Financial Impact of Increased Government Deficits, Post-Oil Shock Period

Since 1975, expanded fiscal deficit, in relation to GNP, has become a perennial feature of the economy in both the United States and Japan. (See figure 3–5.) However, in spite of a deficit at least twice the size of that of the United States in relation to GNP, the expansion in the Japanese fiscal deficit has coexisted with a stabilizing trend in domestic inflation. In contrast, a smaller fiscal deficit occurred in conjunction with a worsening inflation in the United States in 1978–1980. Why did the larger Japanese fiscal deficit cause a smaller impact on domestic inflation, while the smaller U.S. deficit was perennially perceived as an inflationary threat?

First, the larger Japanese fiscal deficit occurred in the context of a sharper decline, relative to historical standards, in the growth of domestic demand, particularly in the business sector. Business investment remained weak from 1975 through mid-1978 because of a severe worsening in business outlook. The decline in profit margins and net business saving was followed by a sharp cutback in net business investment, resulting in a significant weakening of business loan demand and its claim on the households' excess saving. In contrast, the recovery of business demand, both for productive facilities and housing, was much swifter in the United States following the 1974–1975 recession. (See table 3–2.) Consequently credit demands by the private sector also recovered quickly (figure 6–5).

Second, because of the combination of weak private loan demand and a prolonged pursuit of restrictive monetary policy, the growth of money supply declined much more sharply in Japan than in the United States despite a much larger fiscal deficit in relation to GNP. (See figures 2–5 and 3–1.) Meanwhile, unit labor costs stabilized in Japan because of a marked moderation in wage behavior and a gradual recovery in the growth of labor productivity. In contrast, the increases in unit labor costs accelerated in the United States from 1977 onward because of a deterioration in productivity growth and a lack of significant moderation in wage behavior. (See figures 4–2 and 4–3.)

These factors—the stagnation of business demand, the marked slowdown in the growth of money supply, and the stabilization of unit labor costs—contributed to the stabilization of domestic inflation in Japan despite a larger fiscal deficit in relation to GNP. In comparison, a stronger recovery in business demand, a less restrictive monetary policy, and a worsening in unit labor costs contributed to a worsening of domestic inflation in the United States despite a smaller fiscal deficit in relation to GNP.

A related question is, Did the larger fiscal deficit and tighter monetary policy in Japan cause some crowding out of private loan demand, thereby contributing to a delay in the recovery of business investment demand? Although a definite answer to this issue cannot be given here, the following points warrant attention. First, the saving propensity of households in Japan increased after the first oil shock while it declined in the United States. Partly because of this, the Japanese fiscal deficit, while larger than that of the United States in relation to GNP, actually constituted a smaller percentage of the respective households' surplus saving. The banking sector in Japan, faced with increased household saving and diminished business loan demand, increased the share of government bonds in its asset portfolio partly in response to semicompulsory allocation of bond issues by the government. Nonfinancial business firms, reflecting their weak loan demand, also actively engaged in "Gensaki" trading: the reverse lending of idle business funds to banks or security houses in exchange for government bonds held by them. Thus, between 1974 and 1980, the share of government bonds in the Japanese deposit banks' asset portfolio increased by 6.5 percentage points while that of outstanding loans declined by 7.0 percentage points. In comparison, the share of securities in U.S. commercial banks'

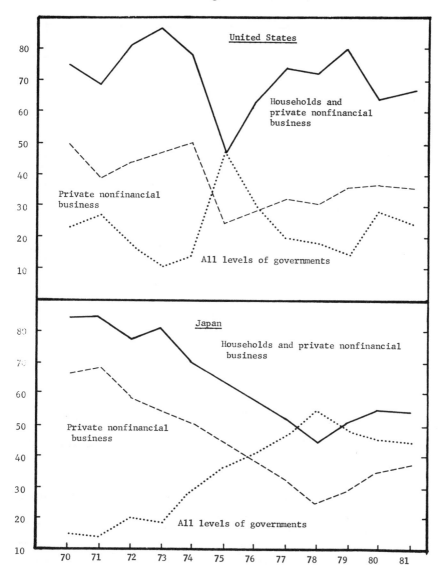

Figure 6-5 Share of Funds Raised in Credit Markets, 1970–1981 (percentages)

asset portfolio actually suffered a modest decline.[13] Second, another evidence of weak loan demand in Japan is provided by the continuing declining trend of key market interest rates (for call money and Gensaki trading) during 1976–1978 (figure 6-6). In comparison, key U.S. interest rates turned up sharply as early as 1977 along with the pick-up of business activity and in-

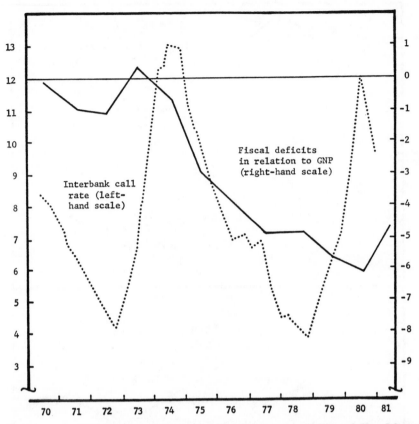

Figure 6–6. Japanese Fiscal Deficits in Relation to GNP and Key Money Market Interest Rate, 1970–1980 (percentages)

flationary trends. The upturn in Japanese market interest rates occurred only from mid-1979 following the outbreak of the second oil shock and the tightening of monetary policy. Thus, the expanding fiscal deficit from 1975 to 1978 appeared to have exerted little impact on the movements of market interest rates and thereby of private loan demand in Japan. In comparison, the rising interest rates in the United States in 1977–1979 occurred in conjunction with rising business activity and domestic inflation but a declining fiscal deficit in relation to GNP (figures 3–2 and 3–5).

Notes

    1. Including about 3 percent for government nonmilitary capital expenditures.

    2. Although varying in magnitude, such a decline was widespread among the oil importing countries. By contrast, the oil exporting countries

experienced a sharp gain in the saving ratio. See my *Developing Countries in a Turbulent World: Patterns of Adjustment Since the Oil Crisis* (New York: Praeger Publishers, 1981), pp. 46, 60–61.

3. Defense expenditure ranged from 13 percent of GNP in the early 1950s to 6 to 8 percent in the late 1960s and early 1970s in the United States. In Japan, it remained less than 1 percent throughout the whole period.

4. A phrase borrowed from Kazushi Ohkawa and Henry Rosovsky, *Japanese Economic Growth: Trend Acceleration in the Twentieth Century* (Stanford: Stanford University Press, 1973). The phenomenon is by no means unique to Japan. Similar acceleration in economic growth rate occurred in Taiwan and several other countries between the prewar and postwar periods.

5. For an argument based on upward shifting of wealth-income targets, see Kazuo Sato, "Why Have the Japanese Saved So Much? On Determinants of Japanese Household Saving" (Mimeo. for presentation at the Japan Economic Seminar, George Washington University, Washington, D.C., January 23, 1982).

6. Although most retirees at age fifty-five try to find a new job, usually with lower pay, there are few job openings available for such job seekers. However, the mandatory retirement age is being extended to around age sixty-one in many corporations.

7. Victor R. Fuchs, "Continuity and Change in American Life," in Martin Feldstein, ed., *The American Economy in Transition* (Chicago: University of Chicago Press, 1980), p. 323.

8. See Organization for Economic Cooperation and Development, Working Party No. 1, Economic Policy Committee, "International Differences and Trend Changes in Saving Ratios" (Paris: Organisation for Economic Cooperation and Development, CPE/WP1(81)9 (October 6, 1981), pp. 98–99.

9. Carol Corrado and Charles Steindel, "Perspectives on Personal Saving," *Federal Reserve Bulletin* (August 1980):615–617.

10. Mark Wasserman and Shirley N. Watt, "The Economy in 1980," *Federal Reserve Bulletin* (January 1981): p. 5.

11. These features of Japan's financial system are widely accepted in Japan and most of them are well documented in Yoshio Suzuki, *Money and Banking in Contemporary Japan* (New Haven: Yale University Press, 1980), p. 1.

12. The important role of financial intermediation performed by the Japanese financial institutions is reflected in the fact that two-thirds to three-quarters of Japanese households' liquid assets are kept in the form of currency and bank deposits compared to only one-quarter or one-third of their U.S. counterparts. See table 6–6.

13. Bank of Japan, *Kokusai Hikaku Tokei* (Comparative international statistics) (Tokyo: Bank of Japan, June 1982), p. 22.

7 Conclusions

This chapter summarizes and brings into focus the findings of the preceding chapters, with respect to the experiences of price stabilization in Japan and the United States in the period since the first oil shock.

Divergence in Movements of Unit Labor Costs

Underlying the differing outcomes for price stabilization in the two countries was a divergent unit labor costs situation. Whereas Japanese unit labor costs stabilized to ameliorate the rise in the cost of materials input, those of the United States continued to rise following an initial decline in 1975–1976. The stabilization of unit labor costs in Japan was made possible by a moderation in the rate of increase of nominal wages and a recovery of productivity growth following an initial drop in 1974–1975. By contrast, the moderation of wage behavior was less appreciable in the United States, while the decline of its productivity growth was much sharper.

Factors behind Divergent Wage Behavior

The moderation in Japanese wage behavior occurred without the prodding of large unemployment, although the decline in the growth of domestic demand and output was much sharper in Japan than in the United States. In contrast, in the United States, the moderation of wage behavior was much less appreciable, except under very high unemployment rates (over 9 percent) as in 1975 and 1981–1982. These differences in wage and employment behavior stemmed from the differences in the employment system and unionism in the two countries. The Japanese system, characterized by lifetime employment and enterprise unions in the large corporations, is less flexible for adjusting employment but more flexible for adjusting wage rates. In comparison, the U.S. system, which emphasizes contractual relationships and collective bargaining, is more flexible for adjusting employment but less so for adjusting wage rates. This makes the Japanese economy more conducive to price stabilization under external price shocks than its U.S. counterpart.

Factors behind Contrasting Productivity Trends

The recovery of productivity growth in Japan in the period since 1976 took place despite a sharp drop in the growth of nonresidential capital stock; however, because of an even sharper decline in the growth of employment, the growth of Japanese capital stock, on a per-employee basis, continued to outdistance that of the United States (at the ratio of three to one). The growth of U.S. capital stock per employee declined sharply in the second half of the 1970s, not from a slowdown in the growth of capital investment but from a sharp increase in employment in sectors other than manufacturing.

The resurgence of productivity growth in Japan was most pronounced in the manufacturing sector, where the number of those employed continued to decline despite a remarkable recovery in output growth. The growth of labor productivity was attained, as distinct from the situation before the oil shock, only partly from an increase in capital stock per employee. The other important contributing factor has been a major improvement in output-capital ratio. This apparently reflected a substantial change in the composition of manufacturing output in favor of industries with a high skill and valued-added quotient (such as automobiles and electronic products), as well as a gradual improvement in the rate of capacity utilization. These developments were helped by the maintenance of a high rate of export growth.

Divergence in Saving and Investment Activity

The lag in the growth of capital investment in the United States behind that of employment, which accelerated in the second half of the 1970s, resulted partly from the low saving propensity of its household sector, which worsened under the impact of oil shocks and persistent inflation. In contrast, the saving propensity of Japanese households, which increased during the period of high income growth in the 1960s, remained very strong after the oil shock despite a sharp slowdown in the growth of personal disposable income. Throughout the postwar decades, Japanese households have benefited from a rate of taxes and nontax payments much lower than that of their U.S. counterparts (the differential being around 15 percent of household receipts). The lower tax rate was made possible partly by a rate of government spending for national defense much lower than that of the United States (less than 1 percent of GNP in Japan compared to 5 to 10 percent in the United States during the period under review). In addition, there were strong incentives for Japanese households to save and for their business sector to invest in order to rebuild the capital stock and productive facilities destructed during World War II. This process was helped by active government promotion and a favorable external environment, which allowed

Japanese industry to export increasingly large amounts of manufactured goods in exchange for necessary raw materials, fuels, and technologies. These factors—low tax burden, strong incentives for saving and investment, and a favorable external environment—combined to create a virtuous circle between rapid industrialization-and-economic growth and rising saving and investment. The onslaught of oil shocks and the worsening of the external environment, while causing adverse impacts on business investments, apparently raised the saving propensity of the average Japanese household as they grew cautious facing a future that has become less certain.

Differing Financial Impacts of Increased Fiscal Deficits

The divergence in saving behavior produced a large gap in household excess savings between the two countries. This, combined with a sharp decline in business investments, enabled the Japanese government to expand fiscal deficits considerably (amounting to 5 to 6 percent of GNP) through increased issuance of public debts, without aggravating inflation. In comparison, U.S. fiscal deficits, even though smaller than that of Japan (ranging from 2 to 4 percent of GNP), claimed a larger share of household excess savings. This, combined with a business investment ratio that suffered little decline under the oil shocks, apparently resulted in strong pressures on financial markets, causing short-term interest rates to fluctuate much more widely in the United States than in Japan.

Limitations of Monetary and Fiscal Policies in Coping with Economic Problems Caused by External Price Shocks

In both countries monetary restraints were used as a major instrument to contain the cost-push impacts of the oil shocks while allowing increased fiscal deficits to mitigate the deflationary impacts of large losses in terms of trade. Such a combination in policy tools did not appear to have worked very well because monetary restraints exacerbated the deflationary impacts of the terms of trade loss, thereby aggravating the burden of fiscal policy, and the multiplier effect of the incremental domestic demand created by increased fiscal deficits was limited by a mismatch in the component of increased public demand and declining private demand. Such mismatches, intensified by the basic change in relative price structure caused by the large increase in oil prices, made it difficult to reduce quickly excess productive capacities (such as in nonferrous metals and petrochemicals), which have become uneconomic. The simultaneous tightening of monetary policy by a

large number of countries in 1974–1975 and again in 1979–1980 also exacerbated the global deflationary impacts of the increases in oil prices through
a contraction in intratrade between the oil importing countries, just as the
largely synchronized expansion of money supply in 1972–1973 by a large
number of countries interacted to magnify its inflationary impact on the
world economy.

Need for Labor-Management Collaboration

The enormous jump in oil prices tends to shift the aggregate supply curve
inward and upward, causing the economy to operate at a lower output and
at a higher price level. To avoid the stagflation thus resulting, it is necessary
to stabilize unit labor costs through wage moderation and productivity improvements to contain the spiral of cost-push movements. Since a moderation
of wage demands in the face of an upsurge in the cost of living is tantamount
to a cutback in real wages, it can occur only if it is in exchange for the
maintenance of employment, which otherwise will decline. This can be
promoted perhaps through government intervention in the wage negotiation
process or through the granting of tax incentives (such as a temporary cutback in payroll taxes) to businesses, which will otherwise implement a temporary layoff of workers. The resulting trade-off can help reduce cost-push
spirals, the fluctuation of employment and domestic demand, and the expansion of fiscal deficits.

Promotion of Saving, Investment and
Productivity Growth

Improving productivity under external price shocks is not an easy task, but
the government can aid it by using tax incentives to accelerate the retirement
of productive facilities that have become uneconomic or by avoiding excessive declines in the growth of money supply and domestic demand. In the
long run, moreover, the turnaround of the falling productivity trend in the
United States requires a reversal of the tendency for capital investment to
fall behind the growth of employment. This requires an encouragement of
saving and investment through a strengthening of tax incentives. However,
the reduction of marginal income tax rates without a corresponding cutback
in government expenditures will cause havoc with fiscal balance. The resulting pressure on financial markets and interest rates may stifle investments,
as the U.S. experience in recent years indicates. Rather, the tax incentives
will be more effective if they are directed to business instead of personal
saving and to investments in R&D and productive facilities instead of in-

vestments in general. It is in the growth of nonresidential capital stock, not in housing, that the United States has fallen behind Japan, and it is U.S. industry, not its nontraded service sector, that has borne the brunt of the double pressures of collective wage bargaining and strong foreign competition.

Need for Vigilance

A great deal of patience and perseverance are needed to eliminate the deep-rooted inflationary psychology that has built up over many years of rapid economic expansion; any letups in stabilization efforts may be harmful in the long run. However, one should not forget the power of simultaneous expansion or contraction in an interdependent world. Under the circumstances, there is a danger that the world economy will fall into a deeper recession if we are not watchful, just as there was one for getting into worldwide inflation. Such a danger is stronger today than in 1974–1975 after the first oil shock. Without the United States and the developing countries acting as locomotives for the world economy as before, the responsibility of Japan and other well-adjusted countries is now greater.

The lesson of Japanese success in price stabilization should not be missed. Without a moderation in wage demands and unit labor costs, the burden on monetary and fiscal policy as a stabilization tool is much greater. The result, even if the efforts are eventually successful, is often time-consuming and costly. From this point of view, an improvement in the institutions governing employment and wage determination are called for in our present world of lowered expectations.

Bibliography

General Interest

Abernathy, William J., Kim B. Clark, and Alan M. Kantrow. *Industrial Renaissance: Producing a Competitive Future for America.* New York: Basic Books, 1983.

Bayley, David H. *Forces of Order: Police Behavior in Japan and the United States.* Berkeley: University of California Press, 1976).

Bluestone, Barry, and Bennett Harrison. *The Deindustrialization of America.* Basic Books, 1982.

Eckstein, Otto. *The Great Recession.* Amsterdam: North-Holland, 1978.

Feldstein, Martin, ed. *The American Economy in Transition.* Chicago: University Press, 1980.

Fukutake, Tadashi. Translated by Donald P. Dore. *The Japanese Social Structure.* Tokyo: University of Tokyo Press, 1982.

Hall, Robert H., ed. *Inflation: Causes and Effects.* Chicago: University of Chicago Press, 1982.

International Monetary Fund. *World Economic Outlook.* Various issues.

Krause, Lawrence B., and Walter S. Salant, eds. *Worldwide Inflation: Theory and Recent Experience.* Washington, D.C.: Brookings, 1977.

Lin, Ching-yuan. *Developing Countries in a Turbulent World: Patterns of Adjustment Since the Oil Crisis.* New York: Praeger Publishers, 1981.

Meiselman, David I., and Arthur B. Laffer, eds. *The Phenomenon of Worldwide Inflation.* Washington, D.C.: American Enterprise Institute, 1975.

Nakane, Chie. *Japanese Society.* Berkeley: University of California Press, 1970.

Nonomura, Ukio. *Zaisei Kiki no Kozo* (The structure of fiscal crisis). Tokyo: Toyo Keizai Shimposha, 1980.

Ohkawa, Kazushi, and Henry Rosovsky. *Japanese Economic Growth.* Stanford: Stanford University Press, 1973.

Okun, Arthur M. *Prices and Quantities.* Washington, D.C.: Brookings, 1981.

Patrick, Hugh, and Henry Rosovsky, eds. *Asia's New Giant: How the Japanese Economy Works.* Washington, D.C.: Brookings, 1976.

Reich, Robert B. *The Next American Frontier.* New York: Times Books, 1983.

Thurow, Lester C. *The Zero Sum Society.* New York: Basic Books, 1980.

Tobin, James, ed. *Macro Economics: Prices and Quantities.* Washington, D.C.: Brookings, 1983.

Vogel, Ezra F. *Japan as Number 1: Lessons for America*. Cambridge: Colophon Books, 1979.

Yamamura, Kozo, ed. *Policy and Trade Issues of the Japanese Economy: American and Japanese Perspectives*. Seattle: University of Washington Press, 1982.

Yoshitomi, Masaru. *Gendai Nihon Keizai Ron: Sekai Keizai no Henbo to Nihon* (Contemporary Japanese economy: Profound changes in the world economy and Japan). Tokyo: Toyo Keizai Shimposha, 1977.

_____ . *Nihon Keizai Konmei Kokufuku no Joken: Ikoki no Kaimei* (Prerequisites for overcoming the confusions in the Japanese economy: Analysis of the transition period). Tokyo: Toyo Keizai Shimposha, 1978.

_____ . *Nihon Keizai: Sekai Keizai no Aratana Kiki to Nihon* (Japanese economy: New crisis in the world economy and Japan). Tokyo: Toyo Keizai Shimposha, 1981.

Inflation Patterns and the Stabilization Process

Black, Stanley W. "Policy Responses to Major Disturbances of the 1970s and Their Transmission through International Goods and Capital Markets." *Weltwirtschaftliches Archiv* 119 (1978).

Blinder, Alan S. *Economic Policy and the Great Stagflation*. New York: Academic Press, 1979.

Board of Governors. Federal Reserve System. "Monetary Policy Report to Congress." *Federal Reserve Bulletin* (March 1981).

Cagan, Phillip. "The Reduction of Inflation by Slack Demand." In American Enterprise Institute, *Contemporary Economic Problems, 1978*. Washington, D.C.: AEI, 1978.

Eckstein, Otto. *The Great Recession*. Amsterdam: North Holland, 1978.

_____ . *Core Inflation*. Englewood Cliffs, N.J.: Prentice-Hall, 1981.

Economic Planning Agency. Japan. *Keizai Hakusho* (White paper on the economy). Tokyo: Economic Planning Agency, 1980.

Economic Report of the President. Washington, D.C.: Government Printing Office, 1981.

Federal Reserve Bank of Boston. *After the Phillips Curve: Persistence of High Inflation and High Unemployment*. Conference Series No. 19. Proceedings of a Conference Held in June 1978.

Fischer, Stanley, and Franco Modigliani. "Towards an Understanding of the Real Effects and Costs of Inflation." *Weltwirtschaftliches Archiv* 119 (1978):4.

Fukuchi, Takao, Koichi Ono, and Mamoru Obayashi. "Inflationary Burst and Consumer Behavior." *Economic Studies Quarterly* 31 (April 1980).

Glassman, James E., and Ronald A. Sege. "The Recent Inflation Experience." *Federal Reserve Bulletin* (May 1981).

Gordon, Robert J. "Alternative Responses of Policy to External Supply Shocks." *Brookings Papers on Economic Activity* (1:1975).

———. "World Inflation and Monetary Accommodation in Eight Countries." *Brookings Papers on Economic Activity* (2:1977).

———. "Postwar Macroeconomics: The Evolution of Events and Ideas." In Martin Feldstein, ed., *The American Economy in Transition*. Chicago: University of Chicago Press, 1980.

Gramlich, Edward M. "Macro Policy Responses to Price Shocks." *Brookings Papers on Economic Activity* (1:1979).

Hetzel, Robert L. "The Federal Reserve System and Control of the Money Supply in the 1970s." *Journal of Money, Credit, and Banking* 13 (February 1981).

Howell, Craig, David Callahan, and Others, "Price Changes in 1980: Double Digit Inflation Persists." *Monthly Labor Review* (April 1981).

Hudson, Edward A., and Dale W. Jorgenson. "Energy Prices and the U.S. Economy, 1972-1976" *Data Resources U.S. Review* (September 1978).

Industrial Bank of Japan. "The Advantages and Disadvantages of the Floating Exchange Rate System for the Japanese Economy." *Japanese Finance and Industry Quarterly Survey* (January–March 1981).

Ishiyama, Hideyoshi. *Hendo Kawase Leto to Nihon Keizai* (Fluctuating exchange rate and Japanese economy). Tokyo: Toyo Keizai Shimposha, 1982.

Klein, Lawrence R. "Econometrics of Inflation, 1965-1974: A Review of the Decade." in Joel Popkin, ed., *Analysis of Inflation: 1965-1974*. Cambridge, Mass.: Ballinger, 1977.

Modigliani, Franco, and Lucas Papademos. "Optimal Demand Policies against Stagflation." *Weltwirtschaftliches Archiv* 119 (1978).

Moriguchi, Chikashi. "Makuro, Keiryo Moderu ni miru Nihon Keizai no Kozo Henka to Seisaku teki Imi" (Structural changes in Japanese economy and their policy implications as seen from econometric models). *Keizai Kenkyu* 30 (January 1979).

Mork, Knut Anton, and Robert E. Hall, "Energy Prices, Inflation, and Recession, 1974-75." MIT Working Paper No. MITEL 79 028WP. Revised. Cambridge, Mass.: May 1979.

———. "Energy Prices and the U.S. Economy in 1979-81." MIT Working Paper No. MITEL, 79 043WP. Cambridge, Mass.: August 1979.

Nordhaus, William D. "Oil and Economic Performance in Industrial Countries." *Brookings Papers on Economic Activity* (2:1980).

Okun, Arthur M. "A Postmortem of the 1974 Recession." *Brookings Papers on Economic Activity* (1:1975).

Okun, Arthur M. "Efficient Disinflationary Policies." *American Economic Review: Papers and Proceedings* (May 1978).

Phelps, Edmund S. "Commodity Supply Shock and Full Employment Monetary Policy." *Journal of Money, Credit, and Banking* 10 (May 1978).

Pierce, James L. "The Political Economy of Arthur Burns." *Journal of Finance* 34 (May 1979).

Pigott, Charles. "Wringing Out Inflation: Japan's Experience." *Federal Reserve Bank of San Francisco Economic Review* (Summer 1980).

Pool, William, "Burnsian Monetary Policy: Eight Years of Progress." *Journal of Finance* 34 (May 1979).

Popkin, Joel, ed. *Analysis of Inflation: 1965-1974.* Cambridge, Mass.: Ballinger, 1977.

Quirk, Peter J. "Japan's Balance of Payments: Analytic Approaches to the Experience of the 1970s and Synthesis for Medium Term Projection." Washington, D.C.: International Monetary Fund, DM/79/34, May 17, 1979.

Rasche, Robert H., and John A. Tatom. "The Effects of the New Energy Regime on Economic Capacity, Production, and Prices." *Federal Reserve Bank of St. Louis Review* 59 (May 1977).

_____ . "Energy Price Shocks, Aggregate Supply and Monetary Policy: The Theory and the International Evidence." In Karl Brunner and Alan H. Meltzer, eds., *Supply Shocks, Incentives, and National Wealth.* Amsterdam: North Holland: Carnegie Rochester Conference Series on Public Policy, 14 (1981).

Shimomura, Osamu, *Zero Seicho Dasshutsu no Joken* (Prerequisites for escaping from zero growth). Tokyo: Toyo Shimposha, 1976.

Shinkai, Yoichi. "Is Stabilization Policy Possible in Japan?" *Japanese Economic Studies* (Summer 1977).

_____ . "Oil Crisis and Stagflation in Japan." In Kozo Yamamura, *Policy and Trade Issues of the Japanese Economy.* University of Washington Press, 1982.

Smith, Paul F. "Changing Patterns in the Cycles in Short Term Interest Rates." *Journal of Banking and Finance* 3 (1979):383-395.

Stein, Jerome L. "Inflation and Stagflation." *Journal of Banking and Finance* 2 (1978):109-131.

Suzuki, Takashi. *Nihon Keizai no Henbo to Bukka* (Changes in Japanese economy and inflation). Tokyo: Toyo Keizai Shimposha, 1974.

Tobin, James. "Stabilization Policy Ten Years After." *Brookings Papers on Economic Activity* (1:1980).

_____ , and Robert Hall. "The Reagan Economic Program." Supplement to *Federal Reserve Bank of San Francisco Economic Review*, May 1, 1981.

Wasserman, Mark A, and Shirley N. Watt. "The Economy in 1980." *Federal Reserve Bulletin* (January 1981).

Wenninger, John, Lawrence Radecki, and Elizabeth Hammond. "Recent Instability in the Demand for Money." *FRBNY Quarterly Review* (Summer 1981).

Whitman, Marina v. N. "The Locomotive Approach to Sustaining World Recovery: Has It Run Out of Steam?" In American Enterprise Institute, *Contemporary Economic Problems, 1978.* Washington, D.C.: AEI, 1978.

Wojnilower, Albert M. "The Central Role of Credit Crunches in Recent Financial History." *Brookings Papers on Economic Activity* (2:1980).

Wood, Geoffrey E., and Nancy Ammon Jinakoplos. "Coordinated International Economic Expansion: Are Convoys or Locomotives the Answer?" *Federal Reserve Bank of St. Louis Economic Review* (July 1978).

Yoshitomi, Masaru. "The Recent Japanese Economy: The Oil Crisis and the Transition to Medium Growth Path." *Developing Economies* 14 (1976):4.

Wage Behavior and the Employment System

Baily, Martin Neil, ed. *Workers, Jobs, and Inflation.* Washington, D.C.: Brookings, 1982.

Braun, Anne Romanis. "Three Decades of Income Policy: Reflections on the Role of Income Policies in Industrial Countries, 1945–76." IMF *Staff Papers* 20 (March 1975).

Cogan, John F. "The Decline in Black Teenage Employment: 1959–70." *American Economic Review* 72 (September 1982).

Douty, H.M. "The Slowdown in Real Wages: A Postwar Perspective." *Monthly Labor Review* (August 1977).

Freeman, Richard B. "The Evolution of the American Labor Market, 1948–80." In Martin Feldstein, ed., *The American Economy in Transition.* Chicago: University of Chicago Press, 1980.

Furugoori, Tomoko. "Joshi Shugyo Kodo no Jissho Bunseki" (An empirical study of women's employment). *Japanese Labor Association Monthly* (March 1981).

Hall, Robert E. "Employment Fluctuations and Wage Rigidity." *Brookings Papers on Economic Activity* (1:1980).

Hazama, Hiroshi. "The Maturation of Society and Labor-Management Relations." *Japanese Economic Studies* (Winter 1979–1980).

Kosters, Marvin H. "Wage Behavior and Inflation in the 1970s." In American Enterprise Institute, *Contemporary Economic Problems, 1978.* Washington, D.C.: AEI, 1978.

Kosters, Marvin H. "Wage Standards and Interdependence of Wages in the Labor Market." In American Enterprise Institute, *Contemporary Ecomic Problems, 1979.* Washington, D.C.: AEI, 1979.

Levine, Solomon B., and Koji Taira. "Labor Markets, Trade Unions and Social Justice: Japanese Failures?" *Japanese Economic Studies* (Spring 1977).

Mills, D. Quinn. "U.S. Incomes Policies in the 1970s: Underlying Assumptions, Objectives, Results." *American Economic Review: Papers and Proceedings* (May 1981).

Mitchell, Daniel J.B. *Unions, Wages, and Inflation.* Washington, D.C.: Brookings, 1980.

_____. "Recent Union Contract Concessions." *Brookings Papers on Economic Activity.* Brookings (1:1982).

Moy, Joyanna, and Constance Sorrentino. "Unemployment, Labor Force Trends, and Layoff Practices in 10 Countries." *Monthly Labor Review* (December 1981).

Niemi, Beth T., and Cynthia B. Lloyd. "Female Labor Supply in the Context of Inflation," *American Economic Review: Papers and Proceedings* (May 1981).

Nordhaus, William D. "The Worldwide Wage Explosion." *Brookings Papers on Economic Activity* (2:1972).

Okun, Arthur M., and George L. Perry, eds. "Innovative Policies to Slow Inflation." *Brookings Papers on Economic Activity.* Washington, D.C.: Brookings, 1978. Papers by:

George L. Perry, "Slowing the Wage Price Spiral: The Macroeconomic Review."

Lawrence S. Seidman, "Tax Based Income Policies."

Larry L. Dildine and Emil M. Sunley, "Administrative Problems of Tax Based Income Policies."

Robert W. Crandall, "Federal Government Initiatives to Reduce the Price Level."

Albert Rees, "New Policies to Fight Inflation: Sources of Skepticism."

Abba P. Lerner, "A Wage Increase Permit Plan to Stop Inflation."

Gardner Ackley, Alan S. Greenspan, and Franco Modigliani, "Implications for Policy."

Ono, Akira. "Keizai Kotai to Rodo Shijo." In Kenjiro Ara, ed., *Sengo Keizai Seisaku-ron no Soten* (Controversies over postwar economic policies). Tokyo: Keiso-shobo, 1979.

Perlman, Mark. "Some Economic Consequences of the New Patterns of Population Growth." In American Enterprise Institute, *Contemporary Economic Problems, 1981*. Washington, D.C.: AEI, 1982.

Piore, Michael J., ed. *Unemployment and Inflation: Institutionalist and Structurist Views*. White Plains, N.Y.: M.E. Sharpe, 1979.

Saches, Jeffrey D. "Wages, Profits, and Macroeconomic Adjustment: A Comparative Study." *Brookings Papers on Economic Activity* (2:1979).

Sano, Yoko. "Seniority Based Wages in Japan: A Survey." *Japanese Economic Studies* (Spring 1977).

Shimada, Haruo. "The Japanese Labor Market after the Oil Crisis: A Factual Report." *Keio Economic Studies* 14 (1977).

———, Atsushio Seiki, Tomodo Furugoori, Yukio Sokai, and Toyoaki Hosokawa. *Rodo Shijo Kiko no Kenkyu* (A study of labor market mechanism). Economic Research Series, No. 37. Tokyo: Economic Planning Agency, 1981.

Sumiya, Mikio. "Japanese Industrial Relations Revisited: A Discussion of the Nenko System." *Japanese Economic Studies* (Spring 1977).

Wachter, Michael L. "The Wage Process: An Analysis of the Early 1970s." *Brookings Papers on Economic Activity* (2:1974).

———, and Susan M. Wachter, "Institutional Factors in Domestic Inflation." In Federal Reserve Bank of Boston, *After the Phillips Curve: Persistence of High Inflation and High Unemployment*. Conference Series No. 19. Proceedings of a Conference Held in June 1978.

Waldman, Elizabeth. "Viet Nam War Veterans: Transition to Civilian Life." *Monthly Labor Review* (November 1970).

Capital Formation, Technical Progress, and Productivity Growth

Baranson, Jack. *The Japanese Challenge to U.S. Industry*. Lexington, Mass.: Lexington Books, D.C. Heath and Company, 1980.

Baily, Martin Neil. "The Productivity Growth Slowdown and Capital Accumulation." *The American Economic Review: Papers and Proceedings* (May 1981).

———. "Productivity and the Services of Capital and Labor." *Brookings Papers on Economic Activity* (1:1981).

Bernanke, Ben. "The Sources of Labor Productivity Variation in U.S. Manufacturing, 1947–80." Working Paper No. 712. Cambridge, Mass.: National Bureau of Economic Research, July 1980.

Berndt, Ernst R., and Catherine J. Morrison. "Capacity Utilization Measures: Underlying Economic Theory and an Alternative Approach." *The American Economic Review: Papers and Proceedings* (May 1981).

Capdevilelle, Patricia, and Donato Alvarez. "International Comparisons of Trends in Productivity and Labor Costs." *Monthly Labor Review* (December 1981).

Christainsen, Gregory B., and Robert H. Haveman. "Public Regulations and the Slowdown in Productivity Growth." *The American Economic Review: Papers and Proceedings* (May 1981).

Christensen, L.R., D. Cummins, and D.W. Jorgenson. "Relative Productivity Levels, 1947–1973: An International Comparison. *European Economic Review* 16 (1981):61–94.

Clark, Peter K. "Issues in the Analysis of Capital Formation and Productivity Growth." *Brookings Papers on Economic Activity* (2:1979).

Cole, Robert E. *Work, Mobility, and Participation: A Comparative Study of American and Japanese Industry*. Berkeley: University of California Press, 1979.

Crandall, Robert W. *The U.S. Steel Industry in Recurrent Crisis*. Washington, D.C.: Brookings, 1981.

Daane, J. Dewey, and Samuel A. Morley. "Supply Chic." *Across the Board* (November 1980).

Denison, Edward F. *Accounting for Slower Economic Growth*. Washington, D.C.: Brookings, 1979.

_____ , and William K. Chung, *How Japan's Economy Grew So Fast*. Washington, D.C.: Brookings, 1976.

Ezaki, Mitsuo. "Growth Accounting of Postwar Japan: The Input Side." *Economic Studies Quarterly* 29 (December 1978).

Fallows, James. "American Industry: What Ails It, How to Save It." *Atlantic Monthly* (September 1980).

Federal Reserve Bank of Boston. *The Decline in Productivity Growth*. Conference Series No. 22. Proceedings of a Conference Held in June 1980. Contributions by:

John W. Kendrick, "Survey of the Factors Contributing to the Decline in U.S. Productivity Growth."

Richard W. Kopcke, "Capital Accumulation and Potential Growth."

Ernst R. Berndt, "Energy Price Increases and the Productivity Slowdown in United States Manufacturing."

Robert W. Crandall, "Regulation and Productivity Growth."

Michael L. Wachter and Jeffry M. Perloff, "Productivity Slowdown: A Labor Problem?"

William D. Nordhaus, "Policy Responses to the Productivity Slowdown."

Gordon, Robert J. "The 'End of Expansion' Phenomenon in Short Run Productivity Behavior." *Brookings Papers on Economic Activity* (2: 1979).

Gramley, Lyle E. "The Role of Supply-Side Economics in Fighting Inflation." *Challenge* (January–February 1981).

Hudson, Edward A. "U.S. Energy Price Decontrol: Energy Trade and Economic Effects." *Scandinavian Journal of Economics* 83 (1981).

Jorgenson, Dale W. "Energy Prices and Productivity Growth." *Scandinavian Journal of Economics* 83 (1981).

———, and Mieko Nishimuzu. "U.S. and Japanese Economic Growth, 1952–1973: An International Comparison." In Shigeto Tsuru, ed., *Growth and Resources Problems Related to Japan.* New York: St. Martin's, 1978.

Kendrick, John W. "International Comparisons of Recent Productivity Trends." In American Enterprise Institute, *Contemporary Economic Problems, 1981–1982.* Washington, D.C.: AEI, 1981.

——— . "Productivity Trends and the Recent Slowdown: Historical Perspective, Causal Factors, and Policy Options." In American Enterprise Institute, *Contemporary Economic Problems, 1979.* Washington, D.C.: AEI, 1979.

———, and Elliot S. Grossman. *Productivity in the United States: Trends and Cycles.* Baltimore: Johns Hopkins University Press, 1980.

Kendrick, John W. and M. Vaccara, eds. *New Developments in Productivity Measurement.* Chicago: University of Chicago Press, 1980.

Klein, Lawrence R. "The Supply Side." *American Economic Review* 68 (March 1978).

Maddison, Angus. "Long Run Dynamics of Productivity Growth." *Banca Nazionale Del Lavoro Quarterly Review*, no. 128 (March 1979).

——— . "Western Economic Performance in the 1970s: A Perspective and Assessment." *Banca Nazionale Del Lavoro Quarterly Review* 33 (September 1980).

Mansfield, Edwin. "Technology and Productivity in the United States." In Martin Feldstein, ed., *The American Economy in Transition.* Chicago: University of Chicago Press, 1980.

Mensch, Gerhard. *Stalemate in Technology: Innovations Overcome the Depression.* Cambridge, Mass.: Ballinger, 1975.

Ministry of International Trade and Industry. "Japan's Labor Productivity." *News from MITI*, September 3, 1980.

Nelson, Richard R. "Research on Productivity Growth and Productivity Differences: Dead Ends and New Departures." *Journal of Economic Literature* 19 (September 1981).

Northworthy, J.R., Kenneth T. Rosen, and Kent Kunze. "The Slowdown in Productivity Growth: Analysis of Some Contributing Factors." *Brookings Papers on Economic Activity* (2:1979).

Perry, George L. "Potential Output and Productivity." *Brookings Papers on Economic Activity* (1:1977).

Reich, Robert B. "Making Industrial Policy." *Foreign Affairs* (Spring 1982).

Sato, Kazuo, ed. *Industry and Business in Japan*. White Plains, N.Y.: M.E. Sharpe, 1980.

Schmid, Gregory. "Productivity and Reindustrialization: A Dissenting View." *Challenge* (September 1980).

Strange, Susan, and Roger Tooze, eds. *The International Politics of Surplus Capacity*. London: George Allen & Unwin, 1981.

Tucker, William. "The Wreck of the Auto Industry." *Harper's* (November 1980).

Yukizawa, Kenzo. "Relative Productivity of Labor in American and Japanese Industry and Its Change, 1958–1972." In Shigeto Tsuru, ed., *Growth and Resources Problems Related to Japan*. New York: St. Martin's, 1978.

Financial Intermediation of Saving and Investment and the Role of Government

Aaron, Henry J., and Joseph A. Pechman, eds. *How Taxes Affect Economic Behavior*. Washington, D.C.: Brookings, 1981. Contributions by:

Jerry A. Hausman, "Labor Supply."

Patric H. Hendershott and Sheng Cheng Hu, "Investment in Producers' Equipment."

Roger H. Gordon and Burton G. Malkiel, "Corporation Finance."

Roger E. Brinner and Stephen H. Brooks, "Stock Prices."

Joseph J. Minarik, "Capital Gains."

Frank de Leeuw and Larry Ozanne, "Housing."

George M. von Furstenberg, "Saving."

Charles T. Clotfelter and C. Eugene Steuerle, "Charitable Contributions."

Bank of Japan. "Steps Toward Flexible Interest Rates in Japan." Economic Research Department Special Paper No. 72. December 1977.

————— . "Rising Trend Line of the Marshallian k." Economic Research Department Special Paper No. 74. February 1978.

————— . "General Features of Recent Interest Rate Changes." Economic Research Department Special Paper No. 9. December 1980.

Board of Governors. Federal Reserve System. *Public Policy and Capital Formation* Washington, D.C.: Government Printing Office, 1981. Papers by:

Dana Johnson, "Capital Formation in the United States: The Postwar Perspective."

Raymond Lubitz, "Capital Formation and Saving in Major Industrial Countries."

Martha S. Scanlon, "Postwar Trends in Corporate Rates of Return."

Alicia H. Munnell, "Pensions and Capital Accumulation."

James S. Fralick, "Tax Incentives and Private Saving: Some Policy Options."

Patrick J. Corcoran, "Inflation, Taxes, and the Composition of Business Investment."

John A. Tatom, "Investment and the New Energy Regime."

John H. Boyd and Myron L. Kwast, "Bank Regulation and the Efficiency of Financial Intermediation."

David L. Cohen, "Small Business Capital Formation."

Break, George F. "The Role of Government: Taxes, Transfers, and Spending." In Martin Feldstein, ed., *The American Economy in Transition.* Chicago: University of Chicago Press, 1980.

Buiter, Willem H., and James Tobin. "Debt Neutrality: A Brief Review of Doctrine and Evidence." In George M. von Furstenberg, ed., *Social Security versus Private Saving.* Cambridge, Mass.: Ballinger, 1979.

Carrington, John C., and George T. Edwards. *Reversing Economic Decline.* London: Macmillan, 1981.

Christlelow, Dorothy B. "Financial Innovation and Monetary Indicators in Japan." *FRBNY Quarterly Review* (Spring 1981).

Clark, Peter K. "Investment in the 1970s: Theory, Performance, and Prediction." *Brookings Papers on Economic Activity* (1:1979).

Eguchi, Hidekazu, and Koichi Hamada. "Banking Behavior under Constraints: Credit Rationing and Monetary Mechanism in Japan." *Japanese Economic Studies* (Winter 1977–1978).

Feldstein, Martin. "International Differences in Social Security and Saving." *Journal of Public Economics* 14 (October 1980).

Fellner, William. "American Household Wealth in an Inflationary Period." In American Enterprise Institute, *Contemporary Economic Problems, 1979.* Washington, D.C.: AEI, 1979.

Friedman, Benjamin M. "Postwar Changes in the American Financial Markets." In Martin Feldstein, ed., *The American Economy in Transition.* Chicago: University of Chicago Press, 1980.

————— , ed. *The Changing Roles of Debt and Equity in Financing U.S. Capital Formation.* Chicago: University of Chicago Press, 1982.

Gultekin, N. Bulent, and Dennis E. Logue. "Social Security and Personal Saving: Survey and New Evidence." In George M. von Furstenberg, ed., *Social Security versus Private Saving.* Cambridge, Mass.: Ballinger, 1979.

Kosai, Utaka, and Ogino Yoshitaro. *Nihon Keizai Tenbo* (Japan's economic prospects). Tokyo: Nihon Hyoronsha, 1980.

Kuroda Iwano, and Hoshihara Oritani. "A Reexamination of the Unique Features of Japan's Corporate Financial Structure." *Japanese Economic Studies* (Summer 1980).

Mains, Norman E. "Recent Corporate Financing Patterns." *Federal Reserve Bulletin* (September 1980).

Nishino, Mari. "Inequity in Distribution of the Corporate Tax Burden." *Japanese Economic Studies* (Spring 1976).

Organisation for Economic Cooperation and Development/Working Party No. 1, Economic Policy Committee. "International Differences and Trend Changes in Saving Ratios." CPE/WP1(81)9. October 6, 1981.

Royama, Shoichi. "The Japanese Financial System in Transition." Mimeo., Symposium on Japan–U.S. Economic Relations. March 23–27, 1981.

Sakakibara, Eisuke, Robert Feldman, and Yuzo Harada. "Japanese Financial System in Comparative Perspective." Mimeo. Center for International Affairs, Harvard University, Program on U.S. Japan Relations, 1981.

Sato, Kazuo "The Household Saving Function: The Japanese Case." Mimeo. 1981.

————— . "Why Have the Japanese Saved So Much? On Determinants of Japanese Household Saving." Mimeo., Japan Economic Seminar, George Washington University, January 23, 1982.

Sato, Susumu. "Japan's Fiscal System: An International Comparison." *Japanese Economic Studies* (Winter 1975–1976).

Summers, Lawrence H. "Taxation and Corporate Investment: A q Approach." *Brookings Papers on Economic Activity* (1:1981).

Suzuki, Yoshio. *Money and Banking in Contemporary Japan.* New Haven: Yale University Press, 1980.

_____ . *Nihon Keizai to Kinyu: Sono Tenkan to Tekio* (Japanese Economy and finance: Its changes and adaptation). Tokyo: Toyo Keizai Shimposha, 1981.

von Furstenberg, George M., ed. *The Government and Capital Formation.* Cambridge, Mass.: Ballinger, 1980. Contributions by:

David F. Bradford, "The Economics of Tax Policy toward Savings."

James Tobin and Willen Buiter, "Fiscal and Monetary Policies, Capital Formation, and Economic Activity."

Paul Wachtel, "Inflation and the Saving Behavior of Households: A Survey."

Attiat F. Ott and Jan H. Yoo, "The Measurement of Government Saving."

George M. von Furstenberg, "Public versus Private Spending: The Long Term Consequences of Direct Crowding Out."

Attiat F. Ott and Thomas D. Austin, "Capital Formation by Government."

Patric H. Hendershott and Sheng Cheng Hu, "The Relative Impacts of Various Proposals to Stimulate Business Investment."

R. Jeffery Green, "Investment Determinants and Tax Factors in Major Macroeconometric Models."

M. Cary Leahy, "The Impact of Environmental Controls on Capital Formation."

Edward J. Kane, "Consequences of Contemporary Ceilings on Mortgage and Deposit Interest Rates for Households in Different Economic Circumstances."

Walther Lederer, "The Effects of International Capital Movements on Domestic Production, Investment, and Saving."

_____ . *Capital, Efficiency and Growth.* Cambridge, Mass.: Ballinger, 1980. Contributions by:

Barbara M. Fraumeni and Dale W. Jorgenson, "The Role of Capital in U.S. Economic Growth, 1948–1976."

Dale W. Jorgenson, "Accounting for Capital."

Patric H. Hendershott and Sheng Cheng Hu, "Government Induced Biases in the Allocation of the Stock of Fixed Capital in the United States."

M. Ishaq Nadiri, "Contributions and Determinants of Research and Development Expenditures in the U.S. Manufacturing Industries."

Index

Adam Smith (pseud), 114n
Ara, Kenjiro, 83n
Automatic stabilizer, 47
Automobile industry, 56, 108
Average hours in manufacturing, 79–80

Bank of Japan: 98; discount rate, 42–43, 56–57; role in financial intermediation, 126; flow of funds, 126–127
Baranson, Jack, 113n, 114n
Bednarzik, Robert W., 36n
Blinder, Alan S., 59n
Bonus system: and household savings, 123; and profit margins, 124
Bretton Woods system, 1, 11–12, 97, 100
Brunner, Karl, 9n
Business outlook, changes in Japanese, 44–45

Capacity utilization: 13, 29; and unemployment rate and inventory ratio, 29–30; and unemployment rate, 68–69; and capacity expansion, 102–104
Capital-labor ratio, 91–95
Capital-output ratio: 93–96; inverse of, 93
Capital stock: average age of, 105–106; per employee, 91–92, 94–95
Collective bargaining, 73–75
Commodity shortage, 19
Consumer prices: 4, 19, 24, 26; compared with GNP deflator, 4, 36, 38
Corrado, Carol, 133n
Cost of living, 66, 69; see also Consumer prices
Cost-push versus demand-pull, 3–6, 61–62, 130–132
Currency realignment, 17, 100
Current account balances, 51, 53–54

Data Resources model, 17
Decontrol of domestic crude oil prices, 59
Defect or recall ratio, 110

Defense expenditure: 12, 56; and tax burden, 121
Demand-pull versus cost-push, 3–6, 61–62
Discount rate, Bank of Japan, 42–43, 56

Eckstein, Otto, 36n
Employment: 13; total civilian and manufacturing, 69, 71; of regular workers and average hours, 78–79; by sectors and periods, 88–90; in relation to capital stock, 91–93, 95
Employment compensation: 13; and real output per manhour, 63–65; and changes in cost of living and labor productivity, 69
Employment system: and wage behavior, 72–73; and economic efficiency, 76–81; and worker motivation, 110–112
End of expansion phenomenon, 13
Enterprise union, 72
Excess capacities. See Capacity utilization
Export composition, changes in Japanese, 104–105
Export unit value, 23
Export volume: 51–52; and real output, 16

Federal funds rate, 42–43, 55–56
Federal Open Market Committee (FOMC), 42, 55
Feldstein, Martin, 133n
Female employment, 20–21
Female participation rate, 13–15
Financial assets, household sector, 129
Fiscal deficit, 47–48, 129–130
Fiscal expenditures, 49–50
Fiscal policy, 47–55
Fiscal receipts, 48–50
Fixed versus flexible exchange rate system, 100; see also Yen
Food prices, 17, 19
France, 2, 38
Fuchs, Victor R., 133n
Funds, raised in credit market, 130–131

155

About the Author

Ching-yuan (Ken) Lin is a senior economist in the Research Department of the International Monetary Fund. He is also the author of *Industrialization in Taiwan, 1946–72: Trade and Import-Substitution Policies for Developing Countries,* and *Developing Countries in a Turbulent World: Patterns of Adjustment since the Oil Crisis.*